LISA ST

FOR THE LOVE OF GOD

AND FOOD

CHEF LISA'S JOURNEY TO WHOLENESS

For the Love of God and Food
Trilogy Christian Publishers A Wholly Owned Subsidiary of Trinity Broadcasting Network
2442 Michelle Drive Tustin, CA 92780
Copyright © 2024 by Lisa Stalvey-Coady
No part of this book may be reproduced, stored in a retrieval system, or transmitted by any means without written permission from the author. All rights reserved. Printed in the USA.
Rights Department, 2442 Michelle Drive, Tustin, CA 92780.
Trilogy Christian Publishing/TBN and colophon are trademarks of Trinity Broadcasting Network.
Cover design by: __
For information about special discounts for bulk purchases, please contact Trilogy Christian Publishing.
10 9 8 7 6 5 4 3 2 1
Library of Congress Cataloging-in-Publication Data is available.
ISBN: 979-8-89041-426-7
E-ISBN: 979-8-89041-427-4

I dedicate this book to God above and beyond. He has changed me forever, and now I know that with Him, all things are possible.

My only regret was not coming to Him sooner, but even then, I know He was with me the whole time.

PREFACE

When I published the first edition of this book in 2016 called Food, Sex, Wine, and Cigars, I was much harder and still healing from my wounds than I am now, although I do still have my moments! I wanted to write a second edition of my story as I've matured considerably spiritually, thanks to God, since then.

My intention with this book is to provide support and guidance to those who have experienced trauma, reminding you that you are not alone in your journey. There is no shame in being open about what's happened in your life. Holding that all in only makes us sick over time and keeps us from the joy we all deserve. Life inevitably presents us with challenges and hardships, and it is my hope that by sharing my own experiences and insights, you readers can find solace, understanding, and a sense of connection to humankind. Trauma can be isolating, but through this book, I aim to offer a comforting reminder that there are others who have walked similar paths and have found ways to heal and grow. Together, we can help each other in life's inevitable experiences and find strength in our shared humanity.

ACKNOWLEDGEMENTS

I am alarmingly dyslexic and didn't realize how bad it was until I wrote the first edition. I always wondered why I had difficulty in school, especially with numbers and words, which I still suffer from today. I barfed up a 600-page mess to a published book in 2014. Of course, I wanted to sell millions of copies, but I eventually began to realize it was for my healing regardless of sales, and if the sales were to follow, then that would be a bonus. I'm also quite sure I would have never healed from my crippling anorexia and the many traumas that brought me to this horrible disease in the first place.

Thank you, Beth Dorman-Bearer, for countless hours designing the cover for the first edition of my memoir and for designing the cover for this one, and for little or no monetary compensation except an occasional drink and a few dinners. You've selflessly designed my labels for my gluten-free Butter Barn Butter baking company and finally for designing the first cookbook I've written called The Thoughtful Chef.

Thank you, Frank Coady, my patient husband, for putting up with my moods while writing the first edition of this book. I digressed often into the old ways with my mood and attitude and found myself with no appetite as it was very difficult to look at myself in such an honest way, which included being withdrawn from love. It was a difficult time, but he was supportive of what I needed to do, and for that, I thank you, my love.

INTRODUCTION

I'm Lisa Stalvey, born in the Bethesda Naval Hospital in Bethesda, Maryland (now known as the Walter Reed National Medical Center), in 1956. We migrated to California after my brother was born in South Carolina, where my father was born when I was two years old. My father had big dreams of becoming a composer, which took some time, causing him to read meters during the day and write music at night. I was raised in a creative household full of crazy, misunderstood, self-determining people with their fair share of addictions. No one could tell anyone what to do or how to think, which slowly created a volatile and sometimes abusive environment.

Things were mostly pleasant from what I can remember, but things could quickly turn on a dime, especially between my mother and father. Mom was a concert pianist before meeting my dad in Cincinnati, Ohio, where my father often drove to from South Carolina with his colleagues to play saxophone and clarinet at the local jazz club. My mother gave up her passion for professional piano playing so my dad could pursue his dreams. Years later, he became musical director at Monday Evening Concerts at LA's LACMA, which is still managed by my stepmother today. Later, he founded the Friday Night Jazz Concerts at LACMA as well, which was very successful and alive and well today.

There were plenty of childhood dramas and traumas in my young life, but there were also funny and happy times too, at least from my point of view. I can blame my parents for why things didn't go down the way I wanted them to in my life; that would be a cop-out. But I do have a very selective memory of things, and I discovered of late that my brother remembers a totally different experience from mine! Many of my memories are so completely different from his you'd think we didn't grow up in the same house!

TABLE OF CONTENTS

Forward...8

Prologue...11

Chapter 1: Where It All Started....................................17

Chapter 2: L'Orangerie. The Day Life Changed Forever........25

Chapter 3: Was This The Last Day Of My Life?.................43

Chapter 4: My Encounter With God................................61

Chapter 5: The Surgery & Realization.............................67

Chapter 6: God's Pruning...83

Chapter 7: Returning To Daily Life................................91

Chapter 8: Spago...99

Chapter 9: Jumping Around From Jobs Until It Happened........123

Chapter 10: Bambu..131

Chapter 11: The Malibu Fires And The Northridge Earthquake 1993-1994...143

Chapter 12: After Bambu...157

Chapter 13: The Year I Changed....................................165

Chapter 14: Coming To Jesus..179

About The Author...189

FORWARD

Striving for excellence has been Lisa Stalvey Coady's life-long pursuit. As you read her compelling memoir, you'll see how her talent and intentionality coalesce into remarkable creativity and adventure. This is the beauty of the life Lisa has lived to date.

Is there tragedy? She certainly has lived through trauma. Those challenges shape our being. I came into Lisa's world in 2012 when she had already reached award-winning status as a renowned chef. As someone who has savored Lisa's creative offerings, I can assure you she isn't exaggerating one bit as she weaves this story of redemption.

Dr. Dan Allender states in his book, The Wounded Heart, that we have all experienced abuse, some "big A" and some "small a." Similarly, I suggest we have all experienced trauma, some "big T" and some "small t." Trauma can look like neglect, circumstantial accidents, or emotional wounds from other people's words and actions. Lisa has experienced it all. The glory of her story is how she learned to process her pain. Taking responsibility for how we respond is crucial to walking the path "through the valley of the shadow of death" (Psalm 23).

One of my favorite passages in this book reads:

I chose to go on with my life like nothing had happened. I also felt like I didn't need or want to forgive myself for what I had done. That would mean taking responsibility for what I had gone through.

That was part of Lisa's story, but she turned. She faced her personal demons and found redemption through the cross of Jesus Christ.

I enjoyed Lisa's first rendition of this memoir; I love this one, written twelve years later. Lisa has grown in faith. I met her when she came to receive prayer at Healing Rooms of Conejo Valley in 2012. We had the privilege of continuing her recovery through healing ministry, which included body, soul, and spirit work.

Lisa is a fierce competitor, a genius chef, a loving wife and stepmom (I can relate to the last one), and a fabulous grandmother. She has learned to love herself because she learned to accept the love of God in her life. There is no one who will love you like the Lord God. Lisa now knows this with her whole heart: Jesus is the way to the heart of God.

As you take this redemptive journey with Lisa, my prayer is you will be as fierce in your pursuit of divine healing as she has been. Among the many blessings God has given her, her healing has transformed her into a more creative chef. As a self-proclaimed foodie, I adore Lisa's cooking. I've also had the privilege of going on hikes with Lisa, and her love of God's creation is palpable. She's a gifted artist with a camera and paintbrush as well. We proudly hang a giclée print of a rainbow-colored lion's head in our kitchen; how appropriate is that?!

Yes, our destination is important, but it's our journey to finding God's love that truly transforms us. Lisa's life is a powerful witness to this reality.

Rev. Jill Ricci, M.A.

Author of Awakened To Beauty and Awakened To the Garden of God's Heart

Director, Awakened To Life

www.awakenedto.life

PROLOGUE

For the Love of God and Food takes you on a fiercely intense and intimate ride early on in my life, which was full of unexpected twists and turns; some happy and, for what seemed like forever, sad and painful ones. When I entered the highly competitive and challenging world as a female line cook and eventually an executive chef, I had no idea the possibilities and dangers of what was lurking in the years ahead. I just dove right on in, clueless, determined, and excited. I began my twisted, abusive, challenging, disappointing, and exciting, and to me very successful career, in the restaurant business in the late seventies, eighties, and nineties when women were emerging as line cooks, prep cooks, pantry cooks, pastry chefs, kitchen managers, sous chefs, executive chefs and ultimately restaurant owners.

As kitchens changed and opened up to diners, the image of who manned these stations changed, too. Everyone had to look good, professional, and happy. I started out as a waitress to make money for art supplies, but the kitchen drew me in, mesmerized at the speed with which the cooks pumped out food, the language they used, which was sailor talk on crack, the rawness of how they carried themselves as they didn't need to impress cranky morning customers screaming across the room, "Waitress, get me another cup of coffee!"

I hated that so much that I once deliberately tripped over myself, spilling a hot cup of Joe on his perfectly pressed suit.

moment I decided to give the kitchen a try. The professional kitchen isn't for everyone. You must be tough and watch your back as everyone who was below you in rank was always figuring a way to stab you in the back to grab your station. I never did that to anyone to get ahead. I just did my best work with passion. Those days were wild and crazy times, especially for women literally invading a man's profession, which threatened them like you have no idea. I never got why it was a man's profession when women did all the cooking at home, not to mention managing budgets, kids (if applicable), and pampering the husband when he came from his hard day's work. The practices back then were a moment in time that I highly doubt would fly today, especially sexual harassment.

I started my training at the mature and sassy age of ten, even though I wasn't consciously aware of it until 1978 rolled around. I reluctantly yet welcomed my first line cooking job (which is akin to the front lines in a war) in the largest kitchen I had ever worked in through my entire career: The Good Earth in Westwood, California. That location served anywhere from 1,500 to 2,500 guests a day. It highlighted gargantuan kettles that made gallons of soup each day, a large griddle and grill with fourteen burners, a wok station that had three huge iron vessels that sat on three rings of gas flames each, and a sandwich station across from it that was at least twenty feet long. Whoever worked that station had to be the fastest and most consistent line cook ever. Apparently, I was the fastest as I worked both of them alone, which I'm quite sure was a cruel initiation process to see if I could keep up with the guys. Well, they didn't know what hit them! I killed it, and they didn't like that. They didn't know I climbed trees, ate mud pies, and had mostly boys for friends. I understood the mind of a man early on in life.

I worked the breakfast and lunch service, but not without accumulating a huge pile of shredded lettuce behind me on the floor at the end of the shift. The managers didn't seem to mind, as they would come down to watch me in amazement at the speed at which I made sandwiches. Quickly, I climbed up a very short ladder to become the head cook, throwing me into a world of responsibilities I knew nothing about. Enormous responsibilities were so big that I had no idea how I was going to attack them with the little experience I'd had so far. Then, there were unexpected situations like jealousy from my peers and sexist, misogynistic abuse from the male line cooks, which continued as I moved forward in my career. There were some restaurants that were riddled with drug and alcohol use, which I was totally unaware of at the time because it wasn't on my radar at all. The messing around that happened in walk-ins, dry storage rooms, the backs of restaurants, and bathrooms were also prevalent in restaurants up into the late nineties, when my restaurant cooking came to an end but may still exist. The stories I could tell; I just might as we move on!

Food is sexy, and I think that's because it's hot in the kitchen, and there's so much good energy and sweating oozing around. I've noticed over the years that the types of people who are drawn to professional kitchens and restaurant work, in general, are very special and different kinds of people. Sort of like misfits but highly creative ones, if you will. We aren't built for the corporate world, so we opt to work in a creative space that holds absurd amounts of passion (that's if you were lucky enough to work in really good, high-quality, and acclaimed restaurant kitchens). Even working on the floor as a waiter, bartender, or host was sexy in a way. Some of my line cooks didn't finish high school because they had to go to work to help support their families. Dyslexia, OCD, and ADHD, as well as other learning or focus issues, were absolutely prevalent in the kitchen, actually in all areas of the restaurant business. To follow a conversation or communication in the kitchen, you must have at least one of these disorders or, I like to say, gifts. Some of the most talented cooks I've ever worked with were from El Salvador, Guatemala, and Oaxaca. At Bambu, my last job as executive chef and in the restaurant business was the most energetic and sexually charged restaurant ever. The line cooks were some of the best I'd ever worked with, the absolute backbone of the line. Every week, I would get a recipe from the dishwashers or line cooks from their region, and they would sell like hotcakes. Some of the best cooks on the planet, in my opinion. This is my dysfunctional story in the restaurant kitchen. I've experienced very high-end kitchens and middle-of-the-road kitchens in Los Angeles only (never fast-food places), mingling amongst some of the most famous people in Hollywood and other high-profile occupations along the way.

I was spared working in the fast-food business, and honestly, if I'd applied and got the job and spent one day in any of them, I would have walked out and never told anyone I worked in one.

You will go through at least three painful losses, each of them different yet connected, and all at the young age of twenty-four years old. I discovered the way these things happened in such a short time while writing this book, which is a miracle in itself and more painful to write than the day the accident happened. I thought I had forgiven myself for it all, but I hadn't. I was living the high- life, staying up at all hours of the morning, hanging out at bars after work until the wee hours of the morning, hoping to get attention from men. I needed lots of attention back then and never understood why, as I had a great and respectful relationship with my father. It wasn't until I truly came to God that I started shedding the need for so much attention. I want to be recognized by God now. My validation doesn't come from people any longer, it comes from God, and I am perfect in every way in His eyes.

I met God in the operating room during surgery on Friday the 13th, 1980. I promised Him many things that day, which didn't come to fruition until many years later. I continued to cheat God as long as I could (or that's what the controlling mind of an anorexic thinks) over the following thirty years until I finally hit my spiritual bottom, forcing me to seek God, and it was the best thing that could have happened to me. Fasten your seatbelts and enjoy the ride! My joy, happiness, and purpose come from cooking and making people happy through food, which I believe God gifted me with when I was born. I see now why He "pruned" me the way He did. It was all a part of His plan for me.

1
WHERE IT ALL BEGAN

My career actually began in 1978 in Hollywood, California, by happenchance. At the time, I had no idea that Ma Maison was the hottest restaurant in town. Unbeknownst to me, it generated food enthusiasts, movie stars, and all sorts of Hollywood people and food critics alike which were all A-plus in reviews. Looking back, I feel a sense of pride and gratitude for being a part of such a dynamic and successful establishment. It was the restaurant to go to see anyone who was famous in Hollywood, and of course, the new cuisine by Wolfgang Puck, who I had no idea existed until one afternoon after an audition for a film. It didn't have an address or listed phone number. In fact, there wasn't even a sign on the building. This was my first real apprenticeship. Prior to starting my apprenticeship at Ma Maison, I worked at The Good Earth as a waitress and then became a line cook and finally as head cook in a short year. I then left and went on to The Great American Food and Beverage Company, and that was one dangerous job. They played heavy metal music, offered a four-day work week because it was so crazy in there, wore steel-tipped shoes in case something like a knife would fly by, and, to add to the mayhem, everyone around me was on drugs. I was also in acting school part-time. Every girl dreams of becoming in actress, don't they?

Well, that was a short-lived option, as the day I graduated acting school at twenty-two years old, a producer came over to me and asked if I would like to audition for his movie. I was totally blown away at how fast that happened! Thinking I was on my way to being a star, he took me to lunch the following week, and afterward, he asked me to come to his office to pick up the script. I was so excited as I felt very lucky and blessed to have been approached so soon and at graduation, no less! But instead, he tried to introduce me to the proverbial "casting couch." They forget to teach this little detail in acting school. I resisted and was told if I wasn't willing to sleep with producers, directors, and whoever else to get a job, I would get nowhere with acting. Disgusted and disillusioned, I forced him off and left crying. Disillusioned, I went shopping; that's what I always did when I was upset. I decided to drive down Melrose Avenue—that's where all the cool shops were back then, and saw a quaint, small, freestanding building set back off the street. I drove down Melrose often but never saw this building. It looked like a cute little dress shop, but there were no cars or signs anywhere as to what it was. When I walked in, I found a restaurant. It was very quaint and European-looking. It seemed to be closed as there were no people in it. It was a hot afternoon around four o'clock, so it was probably in between lunch and dinner service. The ambiance of the place exuded a charming French bistro vibe, with a hint of nostalgia in the air. The wooden floor emitted a gentle crackling sound as you walked, adding to its vintage charm, while a subtle, pleasant, old scent lingered in the space. A tall, regal man was standing in the bar area wearing a suit with a red handkerchief in his pocket. He greeted me with his raspy French accent while smoking a cigarette. He introduced himself as Patrick Terrail, the proprietor of Ma Maison. I asked him what the name of the restaurant was. He said Ma Maison and asked me my name. I told him and asked how come there was no sign outside. He said proudly that they didn't need one, and the phone number was also unlisted. One had to know someone to get it. I was quite intrigued by that. He asked if I'd heard of it. I said no and felt a little embarrassed and out of touch saying that. He seemed quite enchanted by me, probably because I was so clueless. He asked me what I did for a living. I said I thought I was going to be an actress up until that day, but after what I went through, I think I should stick to cooking. He asked with a light in his eyes, "You're a cook?"

I said yes and told him where I was currently working. I asked if he'd heard of it, and he said no. After learning what Ma Maison was later from my mom, no wonder we both didn't hear about these places. They were in totally different categories of food. He asked if I'd been to culinary school, and I said no and asked him if I should go. He said no because the chef, Wolfgang Puck, was looking for a line cook with no French training or culinary school. He asked me if I knew who Wolfgang was. Again, I said no, really feeling foolish that I didn't. He seemed to be very amused by my naiveté. He asked what I was doing that night. Was he hitting on me? He had no idea what I'd just been through, and I wasn't going to take this from him either. He had to be at least ten to fifteen years older than me. It was a little creepy to me, but I said I had no plans and asked him why. He asked me if I would come back and have dinner with him and meet Wolfgang for an interview. All I could think of was at that moment that I was definitely supposed to cook for a living. How is it that I randomly walked in for a dress and walked out with a culinary opportunity instead? This wasn't an accident running into him. It was meant to be a part of my path. He obviously knew quite a bit about food and the restaurant business, and that's an understatement. Of course, I said yes, feeling excited, but not nearly as excited when I found out what a gem I walked into. I was going to get this job. I just knew it was meant for me. I was on cloud nine.

***

I got in my ugly brown Pinto and drove home. I hated that car. My dad made me pay for my first car and gave me a budget of $1,500.00, money he was going to use from the Musicians Union. I paid Dad back $50.00 a month. Everyone else I knew in school had fancy cars that their parents bought for them, but Dad made me work for mine, and in hindsight, he did me a great service. He taught me the importance of making my own money and how good it felt to earn it. Thrilled by the invitation for dinner and a job interview, I thought about what to wear. What if this Wolfgang Puck guy was cute? I had to look good, just in case. In retrospect, why did I think like that? Maybe I thought if I looked good, I might have a better chance at getting what I wanted. When I got home, I told my mom what happened, and she couldn't believe that out of all the restaurants in Los Angeles, I drove into the most famous Hollywood eatery to buy a dress, only to get a free meal and a possible job at the hottest restaurant in Los Angeles. But she also wasn't too surprised as she said I always seemed to get things I wanted with ease. She explained in detail how powerful and popular Ma Maison was and how all the "A" listers went there. I decided to wear my Chemin de Fer jeans, Frye boots, a cowboy shirt, and my cowboy hat. Why I felt the need to look like a cowgirl escapes me to this day. I was going for a job interview, not a costume party.

***

It was almost seven o'clock when I drove into the full parking lot of Ma Maison with very expensive cars parked in it. I was praying no one noticed me in my car. When I arrived, Patrick sat me in the bar area, offered me a glass of champagne, and told me that Wolfgang would be out in a minute. I waited about ten minutes, browsing a menu I'd never seen the likes of until Wolfgang came out. Do I call him Wolfgang, Chef, or Mr. Puck? Check out the prices on the menu below! This was considered an expensive restaurant back in 1979. I watched movie star after movie star walk through, and many famous people who weren't in the limelight I recognized at this high-powered restaurant. I couldn't believe I was sitting in such a great place, waiting for a job interview with massive butterflies in my stomach, waiting for a chef I had no clue about. Then I saw him. At least, I thought it had to be Wolfgang Puck walking towards me. He was wearing a perfectly starched white chef's jacket. He was devastatingly handsome. I nearly fainted.

I wished I had worn a dress. He was drop-dead gorgeous. He was tanned, had long hair, and looked like a tennis player. I found myself instantly attracted to him. When he got to my table, he said in his thick Austrian accent, "You must be Lisa. I'm Wolfgang." I stood up and gave him a firm handshake. My dad always said to give a firm yet friendly handshake and to always look the person in the eye while doing it. I remember that handshake well. I had my whole hand then, and I had a firm yet friendly grip, and I could barely say hello without sounding like an idiot. But amazingly enough, my hand is much stronger and has a better grip now than when it was whole! Without wasting time, he asked if I've cooked French food before. I said no, and he said good. He then asked if I liked lobster. I said it was okay, and his answer was priceless. He said I've obviously not had a great lobster before. He said he was going to send me some dishes he is confident I've never had before.

While I waited, I grazed over the menu. Just about every dish on the menu I'd never heard of before. Next thing I knew, a perfectly homemade croissant, which was my favorite breakfast, was stuffed with lobster and finished with two sauces. Beurre Blanc and lobster bisque were placed in front of me. I had never had a fresh, homemade croissant before, or lobster like this, for that matter. Master pastry chef Claude Koberle made the croissant, who I later worked with at L'Orangerie. I can't begin to describe the succulence and sexiness of that dish except that I can still

WHERE IT ALL BEGAN

taste it today. He sent over a few more things, like puff pastry with scallops and caviar and Foie gras with green beans. The duck was served in two ways—one was sliced breast-sliced and the other was a crispy leg and thigh. The veal tenderloin was prepared with sorrel cram sauce of which both were absolutely divine! Many of these things aren't popular today. After this amazing food, Wolfgang sat down with me and ordered us more champagne. He asked me what I thought, and I said (and still can't believe I said this) it was the sexiest food I've ever eaten. He laughed and asked me to come in for dinner almost every night for the next three weeks, with me having high hopes of getting a job while tasting the most sublime food I've ever had in my life in the most famous restaurant in Hollywood.

***

I found myself falling for Wolfgang, but I wanted to work for him and thought I might be able to have both, like most women think, but that wasn't the case. I finally asked him when I was going to start. He said next week, and there it was: my first apprenticeship. I spent the next year, six days a week, learning how to cook the best and the first-of-its-kind cuisine—California French Cuisine. I went home most nights crying as I was making all kinds of mistakes, and it seemed no one was willing to help me. One of my most embarrassing moments, in particular, was when Wolfgang had to leave for a bit and asked me to make a basil Beurre Blanc (white butter sauce, which usually is used as a base to add different flavors) for the John Dory fish as a special. I made it, but it was a dark, muddy green color, and there was no time to make a new one before he returned from a break. So, someone suggested I use a bit of green food coloring. I felt for it and managed to get a few drops on the side of the Baine Marie, totally busting me, plus it was florescent green! Therein began my career of practical jokes and hard work. I somehow bypassed the salad, charcuterie stations, and dessert stations my entire career, except for baking for a brief moment at Ma Maison. I didn't like the tempo of baking. It was too methodical. Everyone else seemed to start there. Why not me?

Wolfgang wanted me to at least see if I liked making desserts. Susan Feniger, who is an amazing chef, taught me some classics, but I soon saw that baking wasn't for me. It was too strict with the measuring and slow-paced vibe of it. The hot line is where I thrived; I loved the heat and was very fast and organized there. Clearly, God gave these special gifts to me, but at the time, I thought everyone had these gifts. I mean, one has to survive on the hot line. Then, near Thanksgiving Day, I heard that Ma Maison was going to be open. At twenty-two years old and many years after my mom passed away, holidays were everything to me with my family. I couldn't imagine not being home helping my mother make the meal. My specialty was the stuffing. Being the naïve little thing I was, I didn't confirm what turned out to be a rumor (or a joke) with anyone and told Wolfgang I couldn't work. He said everyone has to work, and so I quit.

2

L'ORANGERIE, THE DAY LIFE CHANGED FOREVER

It was Friday the 13th, 1980, and an unusually blistering hot December day. Maybe I could blame what happened on this renowned day of "bad luck." I wasn't a superstitious person, but after this accident, I considered that maybe it truly was a day of bad luck. Even to this day, I'm extra cautious on the freeways of Los Angeles, driving in a sea of semi-trucks on the 5 and 101 freeways on Friday the 13th. It also crossed my mind that I might go into a coma in the emergency room or, worse, die in the operating room because I was a skeletal ninety-five pounds (which I didn't know until they checked me in to the hospital)—and being five-foot-four-inch tall and small-boned, that wasn't a good thing.

I looked emaciated, or so Mike and my friends told me. What I saw was a round, plump face that looked like a human chipmunk that had pancakes stuffed in my cheeks. I was happy as a clam as a teen and young adult, doing what I loved to do, which was eating, cooking, and playing beach volleyball. I was at my athletic peak and felt incredibly strong. Then, out of nowhere, I was super thin within a three-month period, and what I saw in the mirror looked very different from me than the way my friends saw me.

Could this be anorexia? I'd heard of it but didn't think I was. Most of my clothes were hanging on me, and I wore a size zero, but I still saw a chunky girl. It amazes me how our mind can play tricks on us and how much it controls us if we let it, which I did. To have seen myself as fat, even though I could see my clothes hanging on my bones, is truly a testimony to how we perceive ourselves when we aren't mentally well. But why wasn't I mentally well? I mean, I truly didn't understand it.

***

The kitchen was run by a fantastically flamboyant chef named Jean Luc-Renault. He wore a rolled-up bandana around his forehead and fluttered about the kitchen whimsically, teaching and showing his crew tricks he'd learned from his French teachers. He wasn't your typical French chef, as he wasn't mean or demeaning to his staff. I'd heard how horrible they can be, turning an otherwise normal line cook into an insecure one. I'd rather die and jump off a bridge or drown in a sea of lobsters pinching me to death before I'd continue to work for a despicable, insecure chef, therefore turning me into one, and that wasn't going to happen! Jean-Luc wasn't that person. He encouraged us to be our best and was also patient and an excellent chef. He also kept telling me to use a wooden spoon in the food processor, not my hand like I rebelliously did. I worked the hot line, as usual, bypassing the pantry and dessert stations. Each line cook was responsible for preparing many things in their stations, which we were taught to keep organized, clean at all times, and well stocked, sort of like running our own mini restaurant. There was this dish called "Eggs Caviar," which was the most amazing dish I'd ever tasted, besides that poached lobster gently lying all snuggled in a homemade croissant with lobster bisque and Beurre Blanc sauce we served at my first serious cooking job, Ma Maison. That had to be one of the top five dishes. I can still taste that dish for forty-five years. "Eggs Caviar" was L'Orangeries' most famous dish. They were served in its eggshell, but not before removing the membrane first, before filling it with creamy scrambled eggs mixed with shallots, cream, and chives, then topped off with caviar. In addition to those and other dishes, I was responsible for making fresh pasta as the special every day.

**

When I arrived at work, I was forty-five minutes late because of that LA traffic we all love so dearly. I was still hungry, so I went straight to the walk-in refrigerator for something small to eat. That shake definitely didn't do the job. Shocking. I grabbed a tiny crab apple to nibble on until staff dinner. But oddly, I had tons of energy. It seemed to me that the less I ate as time went on, the more I felt weird and erratic energy, like I wasn't grounded. That, coupled with the emptiness I felt, a feeling I had started to crave, was slowly beginning to wear me down. It was the holiday season, and we were serving festive dishes like duck rillettes with baked crab apples drizzled with maple syrup and served with celery root puree. Potato Dauphinoise, a traditional French version of our American scalloped potatoes, was always served. The French onion soup was served year-round but sold the best over the holidays. The duck fat potatoes were to die for, my absolute favorite, and so was the Cassoulet—all I have to say is it's divine and my absolute favorite. The walk-in was full of beautiful vegetables, fruits, chestnuts, and meats from Europe. I liked that the produce came in imported wood boxes, giving the walk-in a rustic European feel. It didn't feel like Christmastime, though, because it was so unusually hot outside. It seemed like everything was unusual that day.

As I nibbled on the tiny crab apple, the special pasta I was thinking of making that day was a beautiful Linguini with Porcini Mushrooms with duck confit, tossed with a light demi-glace and port wine-based cream sauce topped with shaved Parmesan cheese. I always created dishes I wanted to eat but never would. As was routine for making the pasta, I put the flour, eggs, and water into the industrial food processor, which was imported from France. Most restaurant kitchens used this type of machine because of its functionality, power, and ease of use. I always considered all machines perfect, thinking they could never be faulty or dangerous, which is ridiculous because a human designed and built them! Just as I began to make the pasta dough, the Virgini and her husband, Gerard, came into the kitchen and called me over to have a word with me. I remember thinking how out of the ordinary that was, especially Virgini.

Again, almost everything was turning into lots of

unordinary events as the day wore on. She never came to the restaurant early and hardly came into the kitchen unless it was during dinner service, usually to ask where the food was for a table and so on. Her tone was panicked and concerned. She told me I looked weird. I told her I wasn't tired. I have no idea how I heard the word tired, but she said that I didn't look tired, but weird. I was confused by what she was saying, as it was so random and out of nowhere, but I did feel off. I insisted I was fine, but she continued to say how I looked off and wanted me to go home. Again, that word, "off." Not only was this a bizarre request, but I also wasn't listening to what she was really saying, if anything.

Did she even understand why she was telling me this? In denial and disturbed, I asked her if she was going to pay me to go home as I couldn't afford to not work. Like missing forty-eight dollars was going to make or break me, but at the time, I thought it might. She said no, and I told her I was staying and that I was just fine. If I had my head about me and wasn't in denial of the disease, which I didn't know I had, I should have asked her exactly why she was telling me this and why I looked weird and odd, but I didn't. I was too proud. Nothing was ever wrong with me. I was perfect. Sense the sarcasm? Instead, she asked me to please be careful, that I looked peculiar and couldn't really explain it. Well, at least she explained herself, but again, I reassured her I was fine and went back to work. Famous last words. I should have taken a moment to think about why she was pushing me to leave incessantly and how abnormal and out of context that conversation really was. She really couldn't tell me either, which should have made me seriously believe what she was saying, especially since she was at the restaurant at a very uncommon time. I now see I was rationalizing this whole moment as me being in a starved state of mind, causing me to not understand where this was coming from. I was a mess. In retrospect, it was so random that in a normal state of mind, I should have run right out the back door and driven home. But I chose to ignore her warning (as well as my own warnings) and stayed to work. But in my defense, who would have thought in a million years that what happened in the next few minutes could have possibly happened? No one.

The really dangerous thing about this disease and, frankly, most addiction-related diseases is that not only is the body malnourished, so is the brain. I experienced a real premonition from her and ignored it. After that bizarre conversation, I resumed making the dough by pulsing the machine for about a minute to get the dough into a meal-like texture. I added some water, and knowing the mixture would stick to the bottom of the plastic bowl, I turned the machine off and removed the lid to scrape the sticky mixture off the bottom as per usual with my hand. Then the vibe, or whatever you want to call it, that Virgini was feeling, unfortunately, became my unforgiving reality. As I tossed the ingredients around the bottom of the machine's plastic bowl, it suddenly and without warning turned on for a split second, with my hand at the bottom of it. There was a pause—a short space in time where everything stopped, as though I had completely missed a second of my life. I heard and felt a thudding sound, the same kind of sound you'd hear if your car ran over a small animal. Immediately, I thought, What just happened to me?

I couldn't hear or feel anything. Everything was moving in slow motion; I felt like I was in a tunnel, watching my co-workers running towards me, asking me what happened. I must have screamed. The experience was similar to what I would imagine a bad car accident might feel like. My hand, at that point, was out of the machine and in my apron. Latifa, a beautiful and strong French woman who was a fellow line cook and still is my friend today, calmly asked if she could see my hand. I said no. I wanted to look first. She said I was being absurd and begged me to please let her look first, as she thought it would be too upsetting for me to see. It was my hand, and I had every right to see it first. I swear, to this day, I have no idea how I found the courage to look at it myself. As upsetting as everything was, I was strangely articulate and coherent. As I opened my apron to look at my hand, I was shocked to see that I was missing some fingers. I was too petrified to look closely at which ones were gone, but it looked like my second, third, and fourth fingers, and I also noticed that my little finger was dangling, barely hanging on by a thread, or should I say a tendon. The freak out I was going through is inexplicable. Just like that, my body changed forever. I was only twenty-four years old and had my whole life ahead of me. Now what was going to happen to me? I had huge dreams and expectations for myself, like a cooking show, for instance. Who is going to watch an amputee on television? I thought my career was over. How was I going to hold a knife if they couldn't fix my pinky finger? I was now an amputee. What was I going to do about that? How on God's earth was I going to live with it? I was perfect, and then I wasn't. My ego and pride reared their ugly heads. I had no idea until that moment how vain and superficial I had become. I was going to have a hard time dealing with this. I knew that much.

***

So much was going through my head, but it all seemed to be going by slowly, even though it was only several seconds of time. That's how fast my mind was moving. Dying before or during surgery suddenly became very real to me because I was way too thin and consumed only 400 calories since waking up. I wasn't ready to die. Maybe if I'd eaten that sandwich at the gym and listened to Virgini, I would've gone home, and none of this would be happening. I noticed that I'd been feeling "off" all day; even Virgini said so numerous times prior! Why didn't I go home? The strange thing about anorexia is that starving yourself is close to what it's like to be high, and I think I was higher than usual that day. Now I see that. I wanted a big, fat, juicy hamburger right then. This accident wasn't something I could put a butterfly on or bandage. This was the real deal. I faintly remember asking if someone could butterfly them at L'Orangerie so I could stay and work. I remember seeing my blood, veins, muscles, and tendons, yet I wasn't bleeding. The endorphins my body created from being in shock gave me even a higher high than I'd never known before. Even when I dropped acid the one time (more on the later), it didn't feel the same as I was feeling at that moment. It was much more organic and powerful. I felt no pain whatsoever, and being a visual person, the image of my hand that afternoon is something I will never forget for the rest of my life. I was feeling a bit faint, too, but passing out in front of my co-workers wasn't an option. I kept telling myself to snap out of it and hang on. Losing control and showing everyone how weak I really was wasn't what I had in mind.

What's really messed up is that I saw myself as weak when I couldn't have been stronger at that moment. But looking back, I wasn't able to control anything but was still trying, something the anorexic needs to perpetuate the disease. If I could have, I would have just bandaged my fingers up and kept on working. That's what I've always done. Once, I burned my arm badly at my first job at the Good Earth Restaurant in Westwood, California, in 1977. I was cleaning the griddle after cooking for almost 900 people breakfast and lunch, and the grill brick slipped, causing it to slam into the upper right-hand corner in a puddle of scalding hot oil, giving me an immediate third-degree burn. I literally watched my skin pop three times, and I'm telling you the truth when I say that it was way more painful than severing my fingers. There was no endorphin rush for that burn. I still thought I could work but couldn't, as the heat that was coming from that burn and the griddle was too painful. I kept it submerged in ice water for four hours before I could brave the drive home, which was only four miles away, but it was very hot out, and it didn't matter how long I kept it on ice!

Little Miss Tough Girl. Don't show pain. Stay in control. It was all about control for me, and I was never more out of control in my life. I realized I couldn't go on working. What was the kitchen going to do without me? I even said that maybe I could come back after they bandaged me at the emergency room! Everyone looked at me like I was insane. I was unquestionably out of my mind. I looked up again as everyone was waiting on bated breath for what I was about to say. I looked up and said in a terrified voice, "Okay, this is really bad. I have to go to the emergency room now." Finally, some humbleness crept in.

***

Latifa, who was afraid of nothing and still isn't, asked again if she could please see my hand. I still said no and that I had to get to the hospital immediately. I told her it was really bad, and I was afraid if I let the pressure off my fingers, they might start bleeding, causing me to bleed out, and the end result would be I might die, and I didn't want to die that day, or ever for that matter. She insisted I wasn't not going to die and asked if my fingers were intact. I told her from what I could see, three fingers were gone and not in my apron (probably stuck in the dough in the machine), and my pinky was dangling. Without missing a beat, Latifa yelled for someone to get my fingers out of the machine. I was told later that Shiro, one of the pastry chefs who I worked with at Ma Maison before L'Orangerie, gallantly went over to the machine and calmly asked someone to get a clean vessel of some kind and to put a lot of ice in it with cold water. He bravely found my fingers in the pasta dough and put them on ice. I am quite sure I couldn't have done what he did that day, but then again, maybe I would've. We can do pretty incredible things when we are forced to.

Meanwhile, Rochelle, another pastry chef, got her car to drive me to the hospital. The disbelief I felt was so intense that it was all I could do not to pass out from unequivocal fear. I came close, though. I truly believed I could get my fingers sewn up in no time and go back to work the next day. It was too much for me to engage in the seriousness of what had happened to me. My co-workers' voices continued in slow motion. The owners came running in to see what had happened to me, but I was already out the door and on the way to the hospital. I remember turning back to look at their faces, especially Virginis', as she foresaw what was about to happen. They looked absolutely mortified. I remember thinking that if she even thinks about saying, "I told you so," and thank God she didn't. I am quite certain I wouldn't have taken that well at all.

As Rochelle chaotically drove down the sidewalks of West Hollywood from L'Orangerie to Cedars Sinai Hospital, I was going into the early stages of severe shock, and thank goodness, because I could feel the pain increasing, but my endorphins were kicking in big time, protecting me from the gruesome, unconscionable accident I just had twenty minutes prior. The fear of what was to come made me sad and sick to my stomach. My mind was racing in a million directions of how this accident could have possibly happened and what this would mean for the future of the career I was planning on having for the rest of my life. I rewound the tragic incident repeatedly and relentlessly in my head. The only thing I could remember at the time was that I was making fresh pasta dough in the large food processor, as I did for eight months and five days a week. What in the world could I have done differently that day than any other day to cause the food processor to start with my hand in it? I felt embarrassed and stupid while my friend and colleague held me while sitting in her lap as I gazed down at my precious three fingers floating in ice water. I began to review the time before I arrived at work, forty-five minutes late to boot, which isn't good on a Friday night "mis en place" (aka prep for my station for the evening), to get ready for the onslaught of a never-ending stream of tickets pumping through the machine.

The morning of the unfortunate accident, I started the day off with the same two hundred-calorie breakfast: a deliberate concoction of measured nonfat yogurt, strawberries,

L'ORANGERIE, THE DAY LIFE CHANGED FOREVER

bananas, blueberries, Muesli, and maple syrup, which I started eating three months before the accident. Why was I measuring food? It was a healthy breakfast for sure, but for me, it was a deliberately measured amount of food, which I always ate from my special six-ounce bowl. I measured, weighed, and wrote down everything I ate and later began documenting all of it in fancy, awesome-smelling leather journals like it was my Bible. Is that healthy for an already lean, mean fighting machine?

My obsessive and self-destructive behavior grew much worse as the years went on and kept me from paying attention to things more important than myself. I gradually found myself compulsively writing down explicit details of what I ate three times a day. Also, I would play three or four hours of beach volleyball and then swim three miles in the ocean before going to the gym to ride the stationary bike for an hour and lift weights—all on a two-hundred-calorie breakfast. After my workout that day, I thought I should order a sandwich as I was hungrier than usual, starving actually, but I ordered my usual protein shake instead. It was 1:30 p.m., and I needed to be at work by 3:00 p.m., and that shake was supposed to hold me over until staff dinner at 5:30. As I drove to L'Orangerie, I felt funny, the kind of funny I think Virgini was trying to explain. I can't really describe it, but I felt off, but immediately dismissed it and went to work, anyway.

Only one other time in my life had I felt this sort of strange feeling. I had a dream when I was nineteen years old. A dear friend of mine and I had once dated briefly, but it ended as he was into Quaaludes. Drugs were not an option for me, even though I found out in many of my relationships that they all were on something. Anyway, I hadn't spoken to him in a few years when he called to say hello, which I found kind of weird. We chatted, and he told me he was going on a road trip on his motorcycle in a few days. Knowing he was still using, I said to please be careful.

That night, I had a dream that he was leaving his house on his motorcycle, high, of course, and has he drove down the street, he drifted off to the right to turn right but misjudged where he was and slammed into a telephone pole. He died soon after on an ambulance gurney, trying to breathe. His lungs finally collapsed, and he died right there. I woke up and called him right away and told him my dream. He thought nothing of it. I was, however, not feeling right about it and feared the worst. The next morning, a friend who also knew him back then called me crying. I knew exactly why, too, and it was the same way I dreamed it. I was devastated. I thought, how in the world did I see this coming? Was this a gift I had and so young? I didn't like this idea if it was true. I didn't want that kind of responsibility. I had some similar things like this happen throughout the years and chose to ignore them.

***

Rochelle was driving like a crazy person, swerving dangerously down the sidewalk, screaming to pedestrians,

"Get out of the way! This is an emergency!" I wanted to look at my hand again to make sure I wasn't bleeding profusely, but Latifa wouldn't let me. I could see spots of blood seeping through my apron, and it scared me to death. Laying my head on her chef's coat, she said in her thick French accent that it was going to be okay. She said I was a strong woman and I would get through this just fine.

Sobbing like a little girl in need of her mother, I thought, why did this happen to me, man? I'm getting married to Mike in two months. Where's my mom and dad? Did anyone call Mike? I looked down and saw the vessel of ice water where my three fingers were floating when a wave of loss came over me like a Mac truck, so it was overwhelming and incomprehensible. I thought, how and who was I going to be now? My fingers had died along with a major part of me as a person. My hands expressed everything I loved to do. Would I see them on my hand again after the surgery? I was convinced that Mike, my fiancé, would leave me because I wasn't perfect anymore, whatever that meant. Worse, if Mike left me because of this, who else would want me? The gloom and doom I was feeling was so deep that I felt like I should go ahead and die. My life felt hopeless. How was I ever going to recover from something this traumatic? The pity party was in full swing, and I was the only one there. Everything I'd worked so hard for over the last two and a half years had come to a screeching halt.

My career was over; at least, that's what I told myself.

Death sounded great right about then, but I was also afraid of dying. I was totally screwed. If I died, at least I wouldn't have to go through what seemed to be most definitely unbearable and difficult. Why did I always have to use my hand to turn the dough in that machine? The chef warned me, but I wouldn't listen. I listened to no one about anything. I thought it was important to touch all the food I prepared. I thought it would make a difference in the way my food tasted. But making pasta dough in a powerful machine and sticking my hand in it was totally stupid, especially after being warned by the chef countless times. Now I would pay for my stupidity for the rest of my life.

I also thought that maybe this accident was literally meant to "sever" my way of doing things up until that point, as I wasn't doing such a great job in my personal and social life. Now I know that God literally pruned me, but I didn't remotely consider this back then. I know now this was a gift, but back then, it was a disaster. He was giving me all sorts of warnings for quite some time, all of which I ignored because I thought I was invincible and didn't believe in God at the time. But coincidentally, I was thinking about Him all of a sudden as I watched my fingers floating in ice water on the floor of the backseat of Rochelle's car. Little did I know, there really aren't any coincidences in life, but actual messages and guidance for our benefit, not harm from God. No matter how violent or gentle those messages are, they are for our best, even if we go through severe pain- both emotionally and physically.

L'ORANGERIE, THE DAY LIFE CHANGED FOREVER

I did believe in something more powerful than me at the time, like apples, crystals, and statues, but why was I so afraid to believe in God?

I was always thinking I was in charge, in total control of my own destiny. As we anorexics learn to shut off the mind's connection to the gut, we also learn to disconnect from people and things. But to be fair, there are many who don't have some sort of addiction who don't believe in God or something higher than themselves, too. I've learned recently that when the brain (Vagus nerve) and the stomach (gut) don't connect, also known as "the two brains," our organs and nervous system don't work properly or at all. I could've been totally disconnected from myself all that time. I thought I was anorexic. Maybe my spine was so out of whack that my brain wasn't communicating with my gut or digestive system. Most babies born back in the fifties were pulled out with forceps, messing with the neck. I was also constipated often. The funnier thing is the way I was eating was actually the ever-so-popular intermittent fasting these days. I couldn't eat really after 3 p.m. as setting up and working in a hot kitchen, there is no time to eat, and we really shouldn't. No way food digests well in that environment. All I know is that I was able to work eight hours in a hot kitchen, play two to three hours of beach volleyball, and swim two miles in the ocean, all on 1,000 calories total for the day.

***

FOR THE LOVE OF GOD & FOOD

3
WAS THIS THE LAST DAY OF MY LIFE?

We finally arrived at the hospital after what felt like an eternity to me. Latifa brought me in, and I knew I was going to soon be alone. That was a displeasing feeling, but I understood it even through my fear. I wondered if Mike and my parents knew about this yet. After all, there were no cell phones to call someone yet. I wasn't full of trust back then, but I wondered if any of the doctors, nurses, or emergency room doctors knew what they were doing and even questioned if they could do it. That, in itself, was insane. I hated hospitals and still do. Hospitals have a two-sided meaning to me; you either go there to live or die, and this sure felt like I was going to die.

I took the health stuff very seriously and still do, but I think I took it a bit too far just to avoid the hospital, and now here I am. Oh, the irony. Latifa gave me a big hug and told me to stay strong, that I was in good hands. If she only knew, the only good hands I trusted were my own, and look where that got me as well! I begged her not to leave. That I was scared I might die. Trying to make me laugh, she said that she was going to have to cover two stations that night because of me. I actually laughed, but she was more than capable of doing it without any problem. She was probably looking forward to it! Still, I felt horrible that she was going to be working her butt off because of me. I stood there at the reception desk watching her walk away, alone and crushed at the idea of what the future held for me. A team of nurses rushed over, put me on a gurney, and rolled me into a partially private room. Once I was situated, I could hear other people behind the curtain dividers, some crying and some moaning. I wondered what had happened to them and felt some bizarre comfort that I was so close to others who were suffering. They immediately plunged what was left of my hand into iodine, and the fingers that were severed went into a big bowl of ice with what looked like iodine, too. I wondered if my almost detached pinky would fall off in the iodine. I wanted to look but couldn't bring myself to do it. After what seemed like a lifetime lying there alone, I began to feel some pain. Subsequently, anxiety crept in so quickly I had no time to think, so I reacted, desperately calling for a nurse as if my life hung in the balance. She rushed in with a sense of panic in her eyes. I asked her where the doctor was, that I was starving to death and wanted the whole thing over with so I could eat, and I needed a pain pill stat. Instead of answering me, they had a slew of questions for me—who to call, if I had eaten anything within the last four hours, if I was allergic to anything, if I had AIDS, and whether I had any psychological problems. I told them I had eaten a crab apple just a few hours before, and to the allergy question, I said I was allergic to codeine, penicillin, shellfish, and, to be safe, anesthesia. Even though I wasn't okay psychologically, I said I was, but I'm sure by my

WAS THIS THE LAST DAY OF MY LIFE?

weight, they knew something was up. I insisted on seeing a doctor immediately because time was of the essence, at least in my mind. Why were the nurses so calm? I mean, my fingers were just severed off in a machine just less than an hour ago. Weren't they worried about me?

One nurse said I was hardly bleeding, and I seemed alert. I asked where the doctor was again. They explained that the hospital was flying in the only highly qualified microsurgeon in the country from Chicago and that he should arrive in a few hours. A few hours? Was she kidding? I'll be dead by then, I told myself. I said what I thought out loud and in a sarcastic tone. One of the nurses said I wasn't going to die, and there would be no way they would let that happen. She also said they couldn't operate on me anyway because I'd been eating food an hour and a half before the accident, and they didn't want me to aspirate. Shocked, I said, "You mean a tiny little crab apple is enough to do that?" In the same sarcastic tone, she said yes, even a tiny crab apple could do that, and not to worry as they were all there if something should happen.

The sarcasm was obvious and annoyed me. At least, that's how I saw it. Wanting to perpetuate more drama, I asked for something for the pain, again, basically pleading. The response was this: "I'm sorry, I'm not allowed." I'm not allowed, and why not? I thought to myself. She was so casual about the whole thing it was disturbing to me, but I should have been relieved, not angry! I wasn't feeling any kind of love or compassion from anyone or anything, even myself. I was feeling so alone and in need of both so badly for what I was going through. When they do what they do for too long, they must automatically detach themselves from all situations so they don't get eaten up alive by genuinely caring for a patient. I get it, sort of. I could never do what she did. I care too much about people and would become emotionally involved with my patients within minutes. She was probably a very caring person, but I couldn't see it. I was so caught up in my own drama. The truth is, I had huge amounts of fear and was so hungry that there wasn't any amount of love or caring that I could've received. I had to shift my focus onto placing blame—and what better place than with her? Sarcastically and in a condescending tone, I said, "I'm hungry, and I'm sure you don't care if I eat, but if I die in there, it will be your fault. I want a hamburger." Looking back, I can't believe how rude I was. And the fact that I had an appetite while my fingers were soaking in iodine in a bowl next to my gurney is astonishing for me to think about today. I actually truly felt I just might die in the operating room if I didn't get something to eat. The nurse said in a clinical yet patient tone, "You know I can't give you anything to eat, and you aren't going to die. I can give you an ice cube to suck on if you like."

Seriously, an ice cube? I pointed out to her that I was clearly emaciated and needed something to eat. That was the first time and the last time for a very long time. I admitted out loud that I was beyond thin. I actually knew I was way too thin, but quickly dismissed that truth after I left the

WAS THIS THE LAST DAY OF MY LIFE?

hospital. She reiterated that I wasn't getting anything and that an ice cube would have to suffice. She kept reaffirming I would be just fine. She left only to return minutes later to tell me the doctor landed early and would arrive in about twenty to thirty minutes. This should have been great news, but the anorexic thrives on negativity. She then told me to sit tight!

Sit tight? Where was I going to go? Jogging? There I was, lying in the emergency room with what was left of my fingers for almost three brutally long hours with nothing to help me with the ever-increasing pain, and she wanted me to sit tight. I was also wondering why I wasn't bleeding after all this time. I started to panic. Were the natural endorphins that were protecting me from the pain starting to wear off? But the facts were I needed some emotional support desperately, especially since my family wasn't there yet. I was hoping they would come before the surgery just in case I did die, just to say our last goodbyes. Then it occurred to me that they were working, and Mike, my future husband, was more than likely playing volleyball, and there were no cell phones at the time. All I knew was one thing: I needed to eat, and that wasn't going to happen at least until the next day.

**

While I waited for what seemed to be yet another eternity, I fantasized about the burger I really wanted. Any burger would have done the job, even a crappy Big Mac

FOR THE LOVE OF GOD & FOOD

or the Jack in the Box bacon cheeseburger that I loved to "chew and spit" so often. This chewing and spitting thing I found out about later is a side effect that anorexics have, which is a disgusting one, but better than bulimia, I thought. I wanted a nice and juicy high-quality third of a pound of ground veal from Vicente Foods Market in Brentwood, California. This is a market that's been around for over seventy years and carries gourmet vegetables, excellent bottled oils and sauces, premium beef, and incredibly fresh and expensive fish. I visualized myself biting into that burger, tasting it as I was building it in my head. I added my two favorite things to the mix: bacon and avocado. As I lay there starving, I could actually smell the fatty aroma of the veal and the bacon being released as it cooked. The smell of bacon always comforted me as a child, and the aroma it released throughout the house as it sizzled made my mouth water every time. Even if I wasn't hungry, there was always room for bacon. My imagination became larger than life. I saw myself pile on the mayonnaise, avocado, bacon, lettuce, tomato, and a thick slice of Muenster cheese that melted slowly on top of it all.

As I created that juicy burger in my head, I bit into it with all the fats and meat juice dripping down my chin; I could taste it—and it tasted divine. At that moment, I found myself so incredibly sad that I had been denying myself these delicious foods that I loved so much over the last three months and only because I thought I was fat. I also wondered, Why in the last three months did I start to do

WAS THIS THE LAST DAY OF MY LIFE?

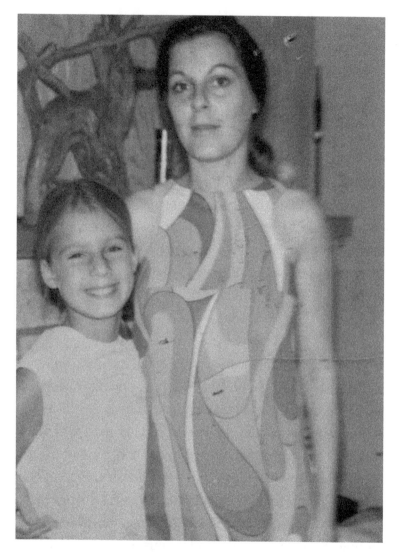

MOM & I WHEN I WAS 10

this? I told God (which was the first time I'd included or even said the word God in any part of my life except, of course, when I was swearing and using His name in vain, which was a lot) I would make the burger I was creating in my head as soon as I got out of the hospital. Snapping out of my fantasy, how could I, as a woman who chose to starve herself, expect to live through a surgery that would more than likely take a long time? It's difficult to explain the plethora of feelings I was going through. I could go on and on, but I felt like a hypocrite. I had spent the last three months starving myself, which would translate into a slow death for some, and now I could die as a result of my accident.

***

I went into another dream-like state, the same feeling I had on the way to the hospital. I felt an urgency to connect with God, but it was out of survival, to be honest. I hadn't completely understood the power of God until way later. I wish I had sooner. I promised to eat normally after I got out of the hospital as I continued to wait for surgery. I was in full fright mode and needed something or someone more powerful than me to step in and save me, but whom was I fooling? I was in deep fear, and promising God that I would eat normally after the surgery was a flat-out lie. Little did I know He knew this, but He continued to love me anyway, even though I didn't know it. I needed Him to keep me alive. I'd heard He performed miracles on lots of people. Maybe He'd give me one even though I wasn't a believer.

WAS THIS THE LAST DAY OF MY LIFE?

I hadn't once thought, cared, or believed in God during my childhood. I believed in the universe pretty much, though, which may have helped save my butt in some abstract way in life up until that accident. I'd heard that prayer could be powerful, but since I'd never given Him the time of day my whole life, why should He answer my prayer now, and how was I supposed to pray?

I said quietly to myself, I'll make a deal with you, God. If you let me live through the surgery, I promise that I will eat like a normal person again. What made me think I could make a deal with God, anyway? This was huge in any case. I was hoping He believed me and would save me. However, I had zero intention of doing what I'd promised God I would do. I just wanted to live. But if He did answer my prayer, and I didn't follow through, what would He think of me then, or worse, what would He do with me after? Would He ever answer one of my prayers again? Has He saved me many times prior to this without praying? I was hoping for a miracle. I had been taking my life for granted on a million levels for a long time. What were the life-changing ingredients I needed to live a more meaningful and fulfilling life? It occurred to me, ever so fleetingly, mind you, that He might have caused this accident to snap me out of the horrible way I was going about my life. Was God actually chasing me and saw I was completely clueless and decided He needed to step in to finally cause me to wake me up? I had no choice but to wait and see if He even heard me or cared.

51

FOR THE LOVE OF GOD & FOOD

***

I began to think about all the things I'd done in the past that definitely didn't align with God's laws. There are too many to talk about, but I'm quite sure they weren't the best choices I've made in my life, like the first time I was with a man, or should I say, a teenager. I was fifteen and a half years old and underage, no less. I knew what I was doing was wrong and felt shame afterward. I had no idea how special and intimate the act of lovemaking really was until that moment, but knowing this didn't seem to stop me from wanting more in the future. To share one's soul with another shouldn't be taken lightly, as I believe now that energy passes on from person to person for life, but unfortunately, intimacy has many levels for all people. Also, that first time gave me a venereal disease. When I spoke with my GP about this, I was with my mom, and if that wasn't humiliating enough, he said I'd contracted the disease about a month before and that whoever gave it to me should have told me they might have it. It could have been treated, but it was too late. I was also facing an unknown amount of time of sterility (which was good news for me), but it wasn't permanent because of the scarring. There was no telling how long they would take to heal (which was the bad news). Still, I continued to have unprotected sex. I must have been a masochist. Still, instead of using that experience as a lesson, I continued to behave the same way for a long while.

Then, at twenty-one years old, I went celibate after

WAS THIS THE LAST DAY OF MY LIFE?

an extremely disgusting experience with a bartender who worked at a popular restaurant called Gladstones on Pacific Coast Highway near Malibu the day after my twenty-first birthday. Not having a relationship with God probably didn't help matters for me, either. I was God. I knew everything. I paved the path I thought I should be on. I was the center of everyone's happiness. Yet, all those paths were painful and lonely. My behavior was horrendous. I was the ultimate alpha female. Lisa the conqueror I was not. I ran around like a free spirit, and as harsh as it is to admit this, I was causing huge amounts of damage to others and myself. To add to the long list of things that happened to me because of my own stupidity, I thought I was immortal, too. I think when we are young, lots of us think this way, but I really thought I wasn't ever going to die. I was so terrified of it.

Obviously, I was starving for attention, which confused me because I was raised in a home where attention was given. It wasn't like I was ignored by my parents, but I certainly didn't plan on contracting a venereal disease. I was immune to everything, and yes, I am being sarcastic. Mortality was a very scary thing to me at the time, and as I've aged and grown closer to God, I'm not afraid of dying. I'd just prefer it to be later than sooner. When my best friend died in a head-on collision when I was fifteen, which was absolutely devastating for me, I saw a glimpse of mortality, but not enough to change the things I knew were wrong for my mental and emotional health. Before this, she moved on to a life of drugs, and because of this, we disconnected, but

53

she was still my best friend. The strange thing was the night she died, I hadn't seen her in months. And she lived literally across the street from me. But, one night, she surprised me by knocking on my front door. I was so happy to see her! She told me she was going out with two of her friends. She hugged me and told me she never had not once stopped thinking about me, loved me very much, and wanted me to always remember that. I told her the same, and then, only hours later, she died. It was surreal. I was so destroyed; when I found out, I couldn't speak. I have no idea if she was high or if she'd been drinking, but regardless, it was as painful as could be for me. I was a frightened teenager after this experience for quite some time, afraid I wouldn't get enough time to do everything I wanted to do in this life because of what happened to them.

***

As I waited for the doctor, I felt like my issues with men or eating issues had nothing to do with my father or mother—at least, I didn't think they did. They gave me tons of independence, maybe too much, but they knew they couldn't control me. But, at the same time, they seemed to care very little about my interests if they didn't coincide with their own, like volleyball or the music I liked, especially disco, house, and techno music, mostly to dance to, but also loved rock and roll to listen to. They never supported me by coming to the volleyball tournaments and dance contests I was in at various clubs around Los Angeles. They never saw how important volleyball and dancing were to me.

WAS THIS THE LAST DAY OF MY LIFE?

Maybe that hurt me more than I realized. Who knows?

Sports and physical activity gave me confidence, that much I did know. Maybe that's why I liked sex so much— just for the sport of it. Knowing better and still not having the courage to make better choices, I continued to make those same bad choices. Cooking seemed to be the only good choice I was making. I also wondered how I was going to break free from these destructive behavior patterns I'd created for myself, which in such a short amount of time had caused me such great pain. The sad truth was that the pain and hurt I created was all on me. Placing blame is a favorite pastime of humans, I think. It felt good to me, yet it felt just as bad. I had created a bizarre type of victimization for myself, fueling my eating disorder. My mind was spinning with memories and questions I desperately needed answers to, and I wanted them immediately. That was who I was then—wanting answers now, not yesterday. I had no patience either and didn't for a very long time after. I had no idea what was going to happen to my fingers or to me, and that alone was inexplicable to me. I had no choice but to let go of the outcome, but this was a stupid hope that didn't exist.

Finally, the doctor arrived. He had no idea what he was about to deal with. My hunger had turned into anger and gripping fear. He introduced himself as Dr. Handel. Seriously? The word "hand" was really in his name? It was almost funny to me, but I couldn't indulge in the incredible coincidence of hand being in his last name. He asked me how I was doing. How am I doing? Being as sarcastic as I could, I told him I was just fabulous, and this was how I was planning on spending my Friday night. A little taken aback, he applauded me by saying he was happy to see I had a sense of humor at a time like this and that the nurse would be in to prep me for surgery in a minute. I was in so much pain, which weirdly took almost four hours to achieve, that I subsequently had zero filters that day. I found myself completely powerless to edit my thoughts and feelings and was incapable of trusting anyone to do his or her job, making it impossible for me to be polite or civilized. Thinking I might not be able to do the things I loved anymore, like cooking, painting, or using my right hand again for anything, totally enraged me.

Without self-control of any kind, I reached my left hand out and grabbed this poor guy's crotch with reasonable pressure. I could see in his eyes that he couldn't decide if he should try to pull away from me in hopes of releasing the firm grip I had on him, which would cause him substantial pain. Or just stand there and wait and see what I was going to do next. I said with determination that if I couldn't paint, cook, or draw again, I would squeeze the life out of him. Almost immediately after I said these horrible things, I felt great remorse and guilt that I was hurting the man who had just flown many miles to operate on me and hopefully save my fingers, if not my life. I let him go and began to cry. Shocked and relieved, he yelled for an IV of Demerol and Valium. I just couldn't take the emotional roller coaster and

WAS THIS THE LAST DAY OF MY LIFE?

pain anymore and needed drugs, and I seriously hate drugs. And to add to the nightmare, two nurses came running over to me and spent about an hour—and I am not exaggerating—trying to find a vein to administer the drugs. My veins were so atrophy due to my weight, most likely that they couldn't find a vein large enough, taking what seemed like forever to finally find one. Ultimately, they found a spot—and on my left hand, no less. I was hoping the drugs would kick in immediately, and they did, thankfully. I told the doctor how sorry I was and that I was obviously not myself. Being the understanding doctor he was, he assured me I was going to be just fine.

***

The drugs kicked in instantaneously—and thank goodness, because I thought I was going to lose my mind if I hadn't already. The drugs made me feel fantastic, almost too fantastic, and I truly had no choice here at all. I only dabbled with smoking pot when I was fourteen years old, listening to Led Zeppelin with severe munchies, but I only smoked that stuff because I thought it was cool. I was higher than a kite on this cocktail of drugs and could have cared less if I lived or died. That's how stoned I was. I'd lived a pretty full life, so I thought. If it was my time to go, so be it. But, on the other hand, I couldn't fathom the idea that I'd never see my friends or family again if I did die during surgery. Would they really care if I died?

I mean, I know my family and Mike would be devastated,

but what about my other friends? Maybe for a week or two, they might, but time always takes care of forgetting. Why did that matter to me at that moment? No clue whatsoever. Where was everybody? Mom, Dad, and Mike had to know what had happened to me at this point. The doctor came in and told me he was almost ready to operate and that it would be over before I knew it. I was so high, I actually asked the doctor if I could watch the surgery. I wanted to watch him and wanted to make sure he was doing it right. I truly believed I might have an idea he hadn't thought of. I expressed concern if I was caloric-deficient. He said there were sufficient nutrients and calories being administered into my body along with the drugs. I asked him how many calories exactly were being administered. He said he didn't know exactly, but it was enough calories for the next few hours he promised. I thought we all promise a lot of things during our lifetime that don't work out, and boy do I know.

I had just promised God an hour ago that I'd eat normally after the surgery. How was I supposed to trust God to keep His end of the deal? Further, who was I to even make a deal with God? I had the gall to ask the surgeon how many hours that was going to be, and he said he had no idea how long it would take. He said it would be over before I knew it and that I would be very much alive, that much he knew. How did he know I was going to live? I thought. He's not God. All of a sudden, here I was, the expert, acting like God and I were best friends after not knowing Him for twenty-four years! They gave me a drug to help me

WAS THIS THE LAST DAY OF MY LIFE?

fall asleep before giving me the drugs for surgery. As I was being rolled into the operating room, I started to get very drowsy. I was going to be saturated with Demerol and Valium for God knows how long and thought for sure I was going to be addicted to them afterward. As they hooked me up to the EKG machine, my hand, which was wrapped in zillions of bandages, rolled off the side of the gurney. Suddenly, what looked like a river of blood came flowing out of the bandages. I had this sudden sinking into nothingness feeling—like the floor was dropping out from underneath me. What a wretched way to feel. I thought I was passing out watching that happen, but instead, my worst fear became a reality. I heard the EKG flat line. I was dying—or so I assumed. That was the last thought I had before I was totally out. *I am dying because I'm too skinny. I really wish I had eaten that sandwich at the gym.*

FOR THE LOVE OF GOD & FOOD

4

MY ENCOUNTER WITH GOD

Having been afraid to die my whole life, I couldn't believe it just might have happened, but I was so drugged I couldn't be sure. Was this drug making me feel this way, or was this what dying felt like? As the EKG flatlined, a sense of urgency filled the room, and nurses swiftly ran over to perform CPR on me. In that moment, I felt an overwhelming sensation of detachment, as if I had transcended my physical body and was observing their efforts from a different realm. I was incredibly thin, and it seemed like my already low blood pressure had dropped even further, leading to cardiac arrest. In that extraordinary moment, a wave of elation washed over me, although I didn't fully comprehend what was happening. It felt as if I had been transported outside of my own body, left in a state of pure joy and excitement. This feeling was unlike anything I had ever experienced before, even when I had an allergic reaction to penicillin as a child. I saw three Native Americans outside my window, engaging in a pow-wow and chanting in their native language, repeatedly assuring me that I would be fine.

As I rose from my body, the transition was smooth and gentle. I felt a sense of freedom and lightness, completely free from physical pain and emotional distress. Time seemed to lose its meaning; my fingers were severed, with moments of feeling like eternity yet passing in an instant. I encountered feelings of pure love and light. I wondered if the mistiness surrounding me was the presence of loved ones who had passed away or spiritual beings emanating an overwhelming sense of peace and wisdom. I couldn't help but wonder if Peter or Susie, people dear to me, were there in spirit. My communication with God was wordless, happening through thoughts and feelings, creating a deep sense of understanding and connection. In that moment, I felt an overwhelming sense of belonging and purpose, as if everything was as it should be, and I was part of a grand cosmic plan. The mistiness that enveloped me was warm and comforting, embracing my entire being in a way I had never felt before. I could hear the nurses rushing over to me, performing CPR and using paddles to revive me, although I could barely feel it. It was strange that I could hear their conversations, considering that I shouldn't have been able to hear anything in my state.

In this ethereal realm, I felt a sense of harmony and perfect bliss, surrounded by continuous love, joy, and contentment. I felt an infinite energy that made me feel like I was floating around in a universe-like realm. I was filled with happiness and a complete absence of negative emotions. I saw myself lying lifeless on the gurney while the medical team worked on me for an unknown amount of time. The feeling I experienced was undoubtedly divine, as if my heart was being filled with God's love. I wondered

MY ENCOUNTER WITH GOD

if I was on the verge of death or if this was a place where one goes to be evaluated by God, determining whether one should move on or return. Perhaps it was a place of protection, shielding me from the physical sensations of the medical procedures. I also pondered if this was similar to the state people experience during a coma, where they can hear what's happening around them. I had heard stories and watched videos of people feeling like they were at a midway point, on the verge of going to heaven or returning.

Then, I felt a multitude of arms surrounding me, even though I couldn't see them. The touch was undeniable, providing profound comfort and reassurance. I believed it was God comforting and assuring me that everything was well. The presence and space I was in felt ethereal, powerful, kind, and beyond this world. I questioned why God allowed this experience to happen to me. Perhaps it was a reminder that we all possess this knowledge in the face of death, or maybe it was a way for God to reveal His existence to those who don't believe. It seemed that I had to die or come close to death to witness this. Suddenly, a light appeared in the distance, not a large light, but bright and exuding a sense of mightiness, as if the entire galaxy was about to open up to me. This wasn't me waking up and seeing the light in the operating room; it was something else. It had to be heaven opening up. Within the light, there was a softness, like mist, surrounded by a bright circle of blue light that was almost blinding. I wanted to move toward it, as I had no desire to go back. However, it wasn't easy, almost impossible. Maybe it wasn't my time yet, and this experience was meant to show me that God is very much alive. I couldn't believe what I was experiencing. I began to realize how negative I had become, and if I were to return to my body, I hoped to carry this bliss with me, shielding me from negativity. The energy and consciousness were so elevated that it would be impossible to maintain that level on Earth. Only Jesus could do that. I knew this without having opened a Bible.

Then, I heard a whispering voice telling me that I needed to let go of everything so that God could work on me. Calm and unafraid, I asked if it was God speaking to me. Overwhelmed with awe, I just knew it had to be Him. The depth and resonance of His voice penetrated the core of my being. It left an indelible mark on my soul. At that moment, I wanted confirmation from God, so I asked Him to explain the meaning of letting go, but there was no response. It was only years later that I discovered the existence of God and finally found my way to Him.

After my brief but intensely beautiful interaction with God, I looked closely at that soft, brilliant, and forgiving blue-white light, longing to go past it and into the next realm. I took it all in. It made me feel so wonderful. I prayed some of it would follow me back to earth. Then, I felt a warm breeze brush over me, similar to that of a breeze from the Caribbean Ocean. I thought for sure I was on my way to Heaven after that, but I was so wrong. Suddenly, everything went black. The soft, beautiful, and

MY ENCOUNTER WITH GOD

peaceful light that I was so drawn to and didn't want to leave was gone in a flash. All I could hear was the EKG beeping again. I heard one of the nurses say that it was a close call. Boy, if they only knew how close. Years later, I had a dream soon after I came to God in my mid-fifties.

The landscape I saw was breathtakingly beautiful, with lush green fields, crystal clear rivers, and vibrant flowers blooming everywhere. The sky was a brilliant blue, with fluffy white clouds gently floating by. There were magnificent structures, golden cities with buildings grander and more beautiful than anything on Earth. I was standing in a huge field next to a marketplace where goods were being sold. The field looked like some I saw in videos that actually went to heaven, but for some reason, it came back, perhaps to tell others on Earth what it's like and to let others know God and heaven truly exist. The colors of the grass, the flowers, and the trees were so vivid, bright, and surreal. There were lots of birds and farm animals roaming around, too, with people holding and loving on them. This was, to me, literal heaven, to lay with majestic tigers, lions, and leopards, holding them until we fell asleep. The feeling was bliss, as if God was reminding me of what happened again and what I had to look forward to. He visits me often in my dreams, waking me up in the middle of the night to talk to Him in the early hours of the morning. I so look forward to this day.

FOR THE LOVE OF GOD & FOOD

5
THE SURGERY AND THE REALIZATION

So, the steady stream of Valium and Demerol began. As I slipped into a deep sleep, hoping and sort of not hoping it wasn't me dying again, I still hoped to wake up during surgery. The curiosity was killing me. I wanted to see how it was done. I don't know how far along I was in surgery, but as incredible as this is going to sound, I did eventually wake up. As I opened my eyes, they felt heavy, and I was obviously very groggy, but I saw a big television screen in front of me with an image of my hand on it. I looked over to my right and saw the doctor looking at my hand through a long pair of telescopic glasses into another huge telescope that was sitting on some type of ladder. I looked back at the monitor and said, "Wow, this is so cool!" Everyone in the operating room looked over at the doctor in shock, and after a short pause, the doctor told the anesthesiologist to give me more drugs, stat! As I faded away, I heard Dr. Handel say he'd never seen a more strong-willed person in his life. I really did want to live, though, and it seemed that God wanted that, too.

After it was all over, which was six hours (three hours longer than planned), I woke up to Mike, my fiancé at the time, standing before me, holding a cup of something.

Thank God I wasn't feeling nauseous, and seeing Mike was actually such a relief to me. I was beyond voracious and craving breakfast, something fierce. It had to be early morning the next day, and Mike was so happy to see me and also looked terribly worried, like he'd aged ten years. He said it was 1:30 a.m. and said the surgery was six hours long, the longest six hours of his life. Then I asked the dreaded question, "Were they able to reattach my fingers?"

I could see Mike was fearing what he was about to tell me. He could never conceal his emotions, though, and said in a crackly voice with welled-up tears in his eyes that they couldn't reattach them. They tried to but couldn't. I could see the sadness he felt for me all over his face. I could see that he would have traded places with me in a minute instead of watching me go through something as hard-core as this. I asked why they couldn't reattach them, and when he told me, I was annoyed! It was obvious because I was so thin, my veins were atrophied. I thought how much that sucked and began to whimper with what little strength I had left with loads of drugs churning through my veins. Trying to cheer me up, he said I was going to be able to hold a knife and only because they were able to sew up my pinky. That should have been good news, but it wasn't. I wanted to go back in time and take the advice of Virgini and go home. I mean, losing $56.00 instead of my fingers would have been the smarter choice, but in my defense, who would have thought this would happen to me? I wanted my fingers back the way they used to be, but that wasn't going to happen. I

THE SURGERY AND THE REALIZATION

told him I wouldn't blame him if he left me now that I was an amputee, not perfect anymore. I don't know how I had the wherewithal to say that at that moment.

MOM & I IN 1957

Trying to hold back his tears, he said that was a ridiculous statement and was actually offended I would even say that to him. I asked him my second dreaded question, "How much of my fingers were left after surgery?" I mean, they

FOR THE LOVE OF GOD & FOOD

were so short when I looked at them right when the accident happened. He told me my index and middle fingers were half gone, and my ring finger was very short due to gangrene, and reiterated how lucky I was they saved my pinky. If I hadn't been so thin, they might have been able to put my other fingers back together. We were to be married in three months, but my gut told me it wasn't going to happen (or should I say, shouldn't happen) and that it would be better to wait as I was way too uncertain about so many things. Just thinking about walking down the aisle in a wedding dress as an amputee made me sad. God only knew what I was going to go through after this experience, literally, but this was not the time to talk to Mike about it as I was very tired and traumatized.

When we got to my room, my parents were standing outside waiting for us, looking horribly distressed. I almost felt worse for them than me. As Mike rolled me into my nice private room, I was exhausted and still very high and didn't know what to say. Mom and Dad came over to me, kissed me on my forehead, and gently hugged me. I think they may have aged ten years because of this as well. They told me how so very worried they've been and apologized for not being there before the surgery. I reassured them I was okay and that I'd be cooking in no time at all and fell asleep. My parents were still sitting next to my hospital bed, looking frazzled and exhausted the following morning. My mom looked especially sad, but she had her usual "tough love" armor on, even during this catastrophe. Dad looked

THE SURGERY AND THE REALIZATION

rather annoyed. I wasn't sure if his anger was focused on me or on how this could have possibly happened to his daughter.

***

That morning, I got lots of calls from my friends and colleagues. L'Orangerie said they were sending over dinner for the family and a great bottle of red wine for us to enjoy. Wolfgang Puck also called feeling horrible for what had happened to me. His call was the most important to me. He was my mentor, and was I blessed for that, even though I didn't have a clue how blessed I was. While hanging around with Mom and Dad watching television, I wondered when the silence would stop. I was also wondering when the food was coming. Just then, Virgini and Gerard called to say that my favorite dish was on the way, which was Cassoulet, a poached chicken served in a small casserole dish with a mixture of stewed chicken with carrots, celery, and onions. It had a clean and fragrant smell.

This wonderful recipe had all the qualities of a typical American-style chicken soup—nurturing and medicinal, nature's penicillin. They also sent potato galettes, which is a dish of yummy, creamy, and crispy French-style potatoes. They were also sending over apple tarts made from homemade puff pastry made by Claude Koberle, a famous pastry chef, and to wash it all down with was a surprise wine. Deep down, I was hoping it was my favorite wine—a 1959 Chateau Pomerol, which happens to be one of the best years for French red wines. I also had the pleasure of experiencing this inconceivably magnificent wine several times at the restaurant. I was very grateful for anything that was coming. While we waited for the food to come, my mind was racing with thoughts like how long would it be before I could play volleyball again? I started playing volleyball in my senior year of high school. I was doing poorly in school and thought playing a sport would help me.

I tried out for the varsity team and handled a volleyball like I'd done it my whole life. Even the coach was amazed I had never touched a volleyball before! I actually achieved MVP and a full-ride scholarship at Pepperdine in Malibu. I turned it down for only two reasons: they didn't have an art program, and I was required to go to chapel four days a week (which I didn't like but definitely could have used, no doubt). If I regret any decisions I've made in my life, this was one of them. I also could have used the business education for sure. I continued playing volleyball for five more years when I met Mike, the famous volleyball beach called State Beach. It was my primary form of exercise besides bicycling. How would everyone at the beach react to me? Would they even care—and why would I care if they did or didn't? I barely socialized with them outside of the beach, but I did spend a considerable amount of time with them. I would soon find out who my real friends were, and that was unnerving for me, to say the least. As far as I knew, everyone loved me. Wow, right? How were my

THE SURGERY AND THE REALIZATION

co-workers going to deal with me coming back to work? Would they avoid me? Would they be afraid to ask to see my fingers, or would they act like it never happened? Would I even want to go back to L'Orangerie? I imagined that no one would look me in the eye because they would be too busy following my hand around, and I would hate that. How would it feel to hold a knife again with my three middle fingers halfway missing? And worse, would I be able to set the volleyball for Mike as well as I used to?

***

Depressed and not knowing the answers to any of these questions of deep introspection, I imagined that the pain post-surgery might be worse than the actual accident. I wanted painkillers, but I also didn't. I wanted to feel the pain so I could heal. I have no idea why I knew this was the right way, but it was logical. Painkillers only prolong the pain. I was going to buckle up and go on the ride, and that's what I did. The doc gave me Darvon, which gave me a wicked stomachache, so I threw them all down the toilet. If I was in pain, I took Advil. It was true—I was much stronger than I knew.

Addictions of all types have been around for centuries. Anorexia, drug addiction, alcoholism, smoking, sexual addiction, and overeating, to name a few, have been problems for millions of people. It's all about "medicating" our pain so we don't feel it. But if we crush our difficult experiences in life through medicating, we never heal. I know now that all the stomachaches, constipation, chronic headaches, eating problems, diseases, cancers, lack of emotional intimacy, and many more diseases and other issues are messages from God telling us to deal with whatever it is because it won't go away with medication, and to take responsibility for what has happened in our lives whether it was our fault or not. Forgiveness is a big one, too. I've had several experiences throughout my life where I had to forgive several people without these people admitting they betrayed or hurt me. But to be fair, if it was that important to me to keep that friendship, I would have approached them and hashed it out. And that tells me I really didn't want them in my life after that, as the trust is gone.

So, even if they did apologize, I still would have forgiven them, but I would never let them in my life again. Some were very difficult ones, but I knew deep down that karma works wonders, but it was still difficult to do. Until I came to God, I truly didn't know how to forgive and let go. Dealing with pain, old traumas, emotional issues, abuse, etc., can't be fixed with a pill. We must do the work, no matter how painful it is, and it frees us from whatever pacifier we choose in so many ways. Also, it's almost impossible to grow spiritually and to get close to God if we don't do the work. Pain is a huge drag, but not dealing with that pain is far more detrimental both physically and emotionally, and I was in more of it than I realized long before the accident. I looked at every other option for a strong spiritual belief system other than God for many

MY DAD & HIS LOVE FOR MUSIC

years after my experience with God. What else had to happen before I truly understood what was really going on with me spiritually? Well, that was up to me. After all, He gives us free will. Thankfully, I gave it all to God in 2012 and now walk in peace and freer from those deep hurts than ever before. I realize that other people's infliction of hurt on another person is almost always a direct result of how they feel about themselves. Very rarely is it about us. The trick is to know this and avoid these people at all costs.

***

Finally, my dad said something. He asked, "How could this have happened to me?" He didn't understand it. I agreed and said I was surprised it didn't happen sooner. He was mortified at my response and asked me why I said that. I told him I knew how dangerous it was to stick my hand in that machine, and the chef also said to use a wooden spoon when scraping the dough around. I told him I'd been using the machine the same way for the last nine months, but this time, the machine went off by itself, and for the life of me, I couldn't figure out why, and it was torturing me.

Then Dad asked, "Why the heck didn't I listen to the chef?" Actually, he used much worse words that I don't want to repeat. My mom looked over at him with her ever-so-famous evil eye and told him this wasn't the time and that I just had surgery the day before and had been through hell. I started to cry at his words because he was right. Dad said he was sorry and explained he was very upset about this and worried sick about me. "Darned machines," he said (he actually used a more expletive word), which was a typical response when he couldn't fix something or didn't know how to express his feelings. The food arrived, and during dinner, we had the most superficial conversation we've ever had in my life. We talked about nothing but the weather and other mundane things, and in retrospect, it was a blessing. Too many heavy conversations have ensued in my family during my short life so far, so talking about nothing deep was fine by me. I wanted to be alone to figure things out, so I asked my parents to leave. I'm not the type to let things get me down too long. Very bad for the immune system. Our thoughts are so powerful many are unaware of

THE SURGERY AND THE REALIZATION

how powerful and what damage they can do to our bodies and souls.

***

Lying alone in that huge, uncomfortable hospital bed, I began to grasp how alone we all really are and how difficult being a parent must be. The stuff my parents had endured over the years must have sucked for them. How many nights must they have stayed up waiting for me to come home? I can't imagine. Even after a child leaves the nest, the parenting doesn't end, ever. I'm sure my parents never thought anything like this would ever happen to their daughter, and neither did I. Then I began to think about the abortion I had just three months prior to the accident. Until I wrote this book, I truly had no idea how deeply this hurt me. We are born naked and alone, struggling to get out into a very difficult world through our mother's womb. I think that is an extraordinary thing, even though I rejected mine. Women go through so much pain to experience the joy of giving birth to a life. I wondered if newborn babies felt anything as they came out into the world through a very tight canal, screaming their heads off.

Do they feel one way or the other about it, or are they even aware of what's going on? Are they afraid of leaving that safe, dark, liquid place they lived in for nine months only to enter a cold, well-lit delivery room covered in placenta and blood? Do they ask themselves what just happened? Then, it hit me while writing this chapter. I suddenly knew why I had become anorexic. It was a miracle, or maybe this is why God stepped in—to give me the time to realize what I'd done to myself. I watched a video recently on how a child develops, and at forty-five days—the exact time I had my abortion—my child had already started developing a heart. I had no idea it was that fast, and that made me very sad. So much develops in such a short amount of time. I had no idea. I suddenly felt and realized that what I did will never leave me, and in retrospect, the abortion—not the accident—is when I really started changing my eating habits and dropping weight rapidly, but for some reason, I chose to ignore the fact that I had the abortion and used the accident as the reason I was so thin three months later. Of course, this was not the case. This was massive guilt I pushed under the rug, but I couldn't make the connection between how emotionally damaging having an abortion was to me and my developing eating disorder.

I was now suddenly aware that I had a problem, even confessing in the ER that I was emaciated. I didn't for one moment ever allow myself to grieve the abortion. I'd only been with Mike for about nine months when I became pregnant, and obviously, the guilt I was totally unaware of apparently had a profound effect on me. Even after this miracle discovery, I still continued on with my disease for the next ten years. I chose to lodge that nightmare away in the deepest part of I'd-like-to-forget-this-event-ever-happened file, thinking I was healed, which, in retrospect, should have immediately stopped my eating issues. Meanwhile,

THE SURGERY AND THE REALIZATION

the abortion continued to eat me alive, literally. I was in absolute and total denial. I felt shame because I knew what I was going to do about it, and no matter what Mike said, I was getting an abortion, and I felt horrible about that.

But in all honesty, it felt great being pregnant. Back then, and still today, more than ever, people who had abortions were considered bad, uncaring, and irresponsible women, not to mention they were defying God and His most precious gift to women. I knew I wasn't an uncaring or bad person, but definitely irresponsible. I also thought how grateful I was that we have a safer option, and not from some back-alley butcher back in the old days. I was in the same position as I imagine how many women felt and went through non-medical procedures in the not-so-distant past before me: relieved, confused, frightened, and ashamed. To receive disapproval and judgment from others about my decision, including my OBGYN, was also making me not want to talk about it openly, making this even more deeply disturbing and my decision harder, so I decided not to tell anyone except my parents, of course, and Mike. Also, in defense of myself, it wasn't like I woke up one morning and thought I might get pregnant just so I could get an abortion! What a horribly demeaning experience I was going to have!

Believe me, the pain of aborting a child is all on the woman, and that alone is punishment. No matter how you look at it or what you believe, it's still the thing the woman has to go through alone, something between her and God.

I should have been on birth control, even though I knew it was harmful to my body, if not for one reason: knowing my being sterile was very temporary, and my chances of getting pregnant again were very real, even with a condom. What a dilemma I was in spiritually and morally! Not once did I think about going full term to give my baby up for adoption, perhaps to a couple who weren't fortunate enough to have children of their own. And as we all know by now, keeping the child was nowhere near the vicinity of an option in my unstable state of mind because of my fear of puking and getting fat. It was as though no fiber of love and compassion existed in me, but it did, and lots of it, making my decision even more painful, but I conveniently brushed it under the rug. I felt nothing, yet everything. My mother always said to me that I should never sacrifice my dreams like she had—which, of course, made me want to have the child just to spite her. Such a rebel I was. My dad always said to be independent in every way, even when I got married. It was a mixed message from both of them, but I liked that advice. It seemed logical to me. She basically sounded like it was my dad's fault she hadn't accomplished her goals, like he'd put a gun to her head and proceeded to squash her dreams. But I got her on that because I knew I couldn't pursue a career like mine and be the mother I would've wanted to be.

***

After it was over, I felt emptiness that wasn't hunger— it was the emptiness of ending the life of a human being, my unborn child. As I look back on my present, healthy state of mind, this was probably when and why I began

THE SURGERY AND THE REALIZATION

my long journey into denying myself food. Not to say that losing my fingers didn't help perpetuate my disease. It more than likely sealed the deal. My joy was nonexistent, too. Looking back on this time in my life, I feel like every emotion, including my sense of compassion, died inside me when I got the abortion, though I didn't notice it at the time. That's how numb I was. Food also started tasting different to me soon after the abortion, too. It had a strange sourness to it, and it was almost a chore to chew it. I kept spiraling further down into a total denial of who I was as a person and as a woman. I was an erratic and insecure zombie. I didn't dare let myself feel any of it.

I chose to go on with my life like nothing had happened. I also felt like I didn't need or want to forgive myself for what I had done. That would mean taking responsibility for what I had done, and I didn't want to. Instead, I went ahead with my life for a long time, thinking that day didn't exist. This may have been the reason for my long journey into the anorexia world of self-loathing and self-hatred, and endless hours, days, and years of pain. Constantly feeling hungry is a very painful thing. The morning after, Mike and I played volleyball all day like nothing had happened—or at least I did. My invisible guilt rapidly began to eat away at me. I continued denying myself the nourishment I so desperately needed after the abortion and for years after. From September 1980 to March 1981, I went from 120 pounds to 92 pounds. I sometimes think about how my life would have turned out if I'd had both babies. During my time in 1987, while I was married to Mike, I experienced another challenging period that included infidelity plus another abortion. It coincided with the vacation I took after leaving my job at Spago, and I found myself in a state of shame of depression—something I didn't experience with the first one. Also, uncertainty about my budding career compounded my feelings of foolishness. Looking back, I believe this was one of the lowest points in my battle with anorexia and as a human being. The experience was markedly different from my previous struggles, and I recall feeling intense self-hatred during that period. I would have loved living a part of my life through my child's eyes. Of course, I know I will never know what that's like and will always be responsible for my decision. Following the accident, I held onto the hope that someday, I would uncover the true reason behind it. Upon reflection, I am convinced that the machine itself was solely responsible. It had to be the cause, and I would make every attempt to find out.

MY DAD & HIS VW BUG THAT TOOK 4 OF US ACROSS THE COUNTRY WHEN I WAS 5 YEARS OLD

6

GOD'S PRUNING

My eyes were puffy from crying all night. The realization that the abortion was the reason why I was anorexic was enough, but the possibility that the accident was my punishment began to weigh heavy on me. After thinking about my near-death experience, God was literally pruning the beautiful rose He created, cutting off the thorns I had created for myself to bring me back to loving myself as He created me. These were some pretty heavy realizations that I had to ponder and live with. The questions I had were very real to me. Would I really be able to work at the restaurant again and face the machine and my colleagues? Worse, was I still going to want to cook? I'd had such big plans for myself before this happened. I had become addicted to cooking and wanted to be a famous chef, maybe even have my own string of restaurants, a cooking show maybe, and write copious amounts of cookbooks.

But who would want to watch it? No one wants to look at an amputee on a cooking show or any other type of show, especially a chef who lost her fingers in a kitchen accident. They would probably be disgusted at the idea of how I lost my fingers and couldn't watch the show because of that very reason, thinking I was some kind of an idiot to stick my hand in the machine in the first place, somehow discrediting me as a chef. I wanted to be the next Julia Child, which was still a possibility, and thank goodness. I could definitely write cookbooks, maybe even a memoir. Before the accident, I had always wanted to have an extraordinary story to tell someday. I didn't think that in a million years, it might be this! I certainly couldn't possibly imagine doing anything else in life. I finally drifted off to some kind of half sleep but was awakened in the middle of the night after dreaming about something I can't remember, but it triggered another profound epiphany, or was it a message from God?

Since the age of five years, I drew a lot, maybe thousands of drawings, which brought me to the intense discovery of my epiphany related to when I was eighteen years old. I began to obsess over the fact my middle right finger wasn't "perfect." I noticed it had bent to the right a little at the second joint and developed a callousness at the first joint because of so much drawing. I hated that middle finger so much that I wished it would go away. I tried forcing it straight, I tried filing off the callus, but none of it worked. I was obsessed with it, and not in a positive way. I sat up in bed and thought, Oh my God, did I wish for this? I didn't know what to do. I mean, that dream was so specific and real that I realized I may have actually caused this subconsciously. I harbored that hate for ten years, and then boom! The accident happens! It occurred to me while lying there in my hospital bed: Did wishing my finger away actually manifest itself into the accident? Could it be that my extreme hate for that finger had something to do with the accident?

On the surface, I tried to convince myself that it was impossible, but being the metaphysical person I am, I knew that it was totally possible. But I couldn't help but wonder if there was a possibility there was some kind of karma attached to it. Incredible as this sounds, I'd completely forgotten how totally disgusted I was by that finger six years earlier, and the irony is that now that the knuckle is gone forever, I now have three stubs to look at for the rest of my life and at that moment I was disgusted by them. I'd do anything to take back all that self-hate. I really did hate that finger. So, I got rid of it, and then some? Was this possible? I realized at that moment that I better be careful with my thoughts. I knew how powerful our minds are and still do when it comes to mental, physical, and emotional health. But was it possible to manifest it over time? I was very thin and quick, too. Probably, my brain was suffering some sort of malnourishment, and I probably wasn't totally paying attention to what I was doing. I also thought how lucky I was that my pinky finger wasn't completely severed. I was still meant to cook because I was spared my pinky. I wouldn't have been able to hold a knife without it, so what's the lesson?

All I could think of at the time was I was taking way too much for granted. I also needed to change my mindset. I was obviously in a negative frame of mind, and I needed to get a grip on this and fast before I harmed myself any further. I was convinced much later on, when I came to God, that He did indeed prune me, trimming me back to learn to love and nourish myself with an imperfection, no less. He also kept that pinky so I could continue on, but with mindfulness and care. It was time to grow, but I didn't. Afterward, I began to read all kinds of self-help books and books on metaphysics, but not the Bible. There was one in particular: You Can Heal Your Life by Louise Hay. She believes that physical issues are a direct cause of how we feel about our bodies and ourselves.

Surprisingly, what my fingers represented in Ms. Hay's book was right on. According to Ms. Hay, the index finger represents ego and fear. I think my ego was in an unhealthy place, not feeling confident about my talents. But at the same time, cooking gave me a healthy ego, which also included power and confidence, which hardly makes sense. I felt, and still feel forty-five years later, a deep feeling of great satisfaction while cooking and creating recipes, especially in a professional kitchen with all those men around me. I knew I was able to keep up and even do better than them, and of course, performing well without their physical help was a big challenge for me, but I did it—even after the accident. I knew I could conquer just about anything in the kitchen, and since men were a special challenge, it made me want to succeed.

The middle finger represents anger and sexuality. Maybe the anger I was carrying was because my finger wasn't perfect before I lost it, and now, certainly, three nubby fingers were certainly not perfect. I'm also quite sure I was angry at quite a few more things, but this accident was at the forefront. It also represents my creative side. And now that this finger is permanently gone, I wondered, did I kill my creativity too? I should have looked at my old middle finger as an artistic masterpiece, but instead, I was angry it didn't look like a model's hand. And sexuality—was it based on my outer appearance? I needed and sought sex out for a good amount of time, which remains a mystery to me to this day since the accident and the abortion were back-to-back.

The ring finger represents unions and grief. I think my first union was so deeply hurtful to me that I became distrustful and disconnected in relationships. And finally, the little finger represents family and pretending. I always wanted my family to be like the Leave It to Beaver or the Gidget brand of family, but, of course, it wasn't. Ours was anything but close to a brand. All families have their dynamics and problems, and we certainly had our fair share. But looking back, we didn't have it all that bad, even though I thought we did at the time. I did not like the surface of life around me being untidy, but there was plenty of it.

So, I posted some positive thoughts all over my house to remind myself how wonderful I was. This did help, but not to the core, like I feel now with God. It touched on the surface of things but still helped. Then, I started evaluating my parents and how they really were with me. My dad was hoping that I would be a famous artist someday, and when I announced I wanted to pursue a career in cooking, I think Dad was disappointed. I could be wrong, but I remember sensing disappointment from him when I told him that cooking was what I wanted to do for the rest of my life. I felt like he thought I could have done better in my life—but what could be better than cooking? My mom, on the other hand, was thrilled for me. She saw my interest in cooking when I was a kid, and since I took over the shopping and cooking in my teens of my own accord, she wasn't surprised that I gravitated towards cooking. Cooking is a form of art, and the fact that I was creating art on plates and getting paid for it at the same time was excellent. I wasn't going to be the starving, suffering artist (that is what artists did, at least according to my dad). He wasn't rich enough to support my painting and photography, and I wasn't marrying for money. I know. That's a mouthful. But all of this seemed logical to me. I enjoyed cooking, and it was physical, something I absolutely needed to be on the job if it was to be a forty-hour week. Cooking professionally is a total workout, and you get eight hours of it a day if not more. I had the best of both worlds. I got to exercise, cook, and make money! For me, I had hit the jackpot, and there was no way I would ever be sitting at a desk all day. No, sir, that wasn't intended for me. Not one time did I visualize myself sitting all day.

I also realized how uptight a person I was, incredibly defensive and super-controlling. What a burden. Now

GOD'S PRUNING

that I'm in my sixties, I think I may know why. Maybe it was because there was so much fighting in my family as a teen. I was afraid the family would fall apart, so I felt the need to take over everything, like I was going to be able to fix things. No one can change things unless they change themselves, but I certainly gave away a large part of myself out of fear. And the irony of it all is that now that my fingers were missing, I had zero control over them being gone. They are gone forever. Even though I started to learn to love myself, I wondered how I was going to address all of these issues as time passed.

FOR THE LOVE OF GOD & FOOD

7

RETURNING TO DAILY LIFE

It was time to remove the bandages. The fear and anxiety I was experiencing were like no other. Since my imagination is and was limitless, I felt like I was standing at the tip of Meru Peak in the Himalayas, which is the highest peak in the world. Because of my fear of heights, that was the only thing I could think of to express how scared I was at that moment. What a heavy moment that was for me to watch my bandage unfold in front of my very eyes. At the same time, the reality was that I was going to be looking at my "new" fingers for the rest of my life. Even today, when I think of that moment, I feel a strange kind of anxiety when I look at them. I've had to work hard to love them. I looked at my hand, feeling so many things: sadness, anger, loneliness, fear, and pain. But mostly, I felt like a freak. I also felt like a member of my family had died; the idea that my fingers were gone forever was the same as mourning a death. The stitches were black and visible, and my nubs were still very swollen. I thought as I continued on with my life, people were going to notice the stitches and then my fingers. How was I going to hide this?

I was told to be very careful not to hit the ends of my fingers on anything for quite a while. He said it would be very painful if I did. It will resemble the feeling of brushing up against shards of broken glass that are on fire if they touch anything. Again, great news. I asked if I did hit them on anything, would a stitch pop open? Thank God he said no! I asked when I could go back to work. He said as soon as I felt comfortable using a knife and the sensitivity didn't bother me too much. But having said that, he said in about six weeks. At this point, he turned to me and said, "Lisa, I know you're very upset, but you were very lucky to have survived the surgery at all." I knew what he meant by that comment, but what he didn't know is I knew that. There it was, my moment to tell both Mike and the doctor what I saw and experienced. What was the point? I was sitting there in his office, very much alive.

I tried to visualize what my hand might have looked like if he had been able to reattach my fingers. In my mind, they would have looked like Frankenstein's fingers. I could see a maze of stitches and, later on, scars. I can still see the scars at the end of my nubs and on my pinky to this day. I feel stress and numbness in my pinky but not sharp pain because of all the nerve damage. When I make a direct hit with my nubs on a wall or some hard surface today, it feels like a surge of electricity going up my arm, and they throb for a good half hour afterward. And sometimes, I cut them, and that automatically brings me right back to that day. Looking back and having lived with them the way they are for the last thirty-three years, I am happy he couldn't reattach them, but of course, I'll never know the difference. I was so unhappy. I wasn't happy with my middle finger at all, which was ironic because I had hated how bent it was when I was eighteen, and now that it was half gone, I was still complaining about it. What was that about? Was there anything I was happy with on my body or in my life in general? A loss is a loss, and this was no different, but now I would be reminded every day of what had happened to me. They bandaged me up and put a soft cast on, too. Simultaneously, while I had the desire to return to work, I also pursued legal action against the company responsible for importing the machine. My intention was not to seek millions of dollars, but rather to ensure that safety measures were implemented for these machines. As news spread, a powerful law firm approached me, urging me to sue for a substantial sum. However, this would have meant giving up my passion for cooking, which was not an option for me. After a five-year wait with the lawyer I chose, I received some financial compensation, which was a positive outcome. Unfortunately, I made the regrettable decision to squander it all. Looking back, I realize that I should have either saved or invested the money to build a substantial retirement fund.

**

The following week went by quickly, and before I knew it, my occupational therapist appointment was upon me. I was told that I might feel the phantom finger phenomenon that amputees often experience. I felt this phenomenon for the first time when I went to scratch my face one morning. My finger naturally stopped at the point where it would have if my whole finger were there. Instead, I was scratching air. It was an inexplicable feeling. I went on to experience that feeling quite often. I spent a few weeks in rehab for my hand and then had to go to the restaurant to face the machine. I was very nervous, but I was dying to get back to work. When we got there, I cried for a little bit but got myself together and approached it. I started the machine and found the sound was hard to hear, but each time I tried, it was a little easier. Then I started it a few more times after that, and finally, I only heard the powerful hum of the machine.

I wanted to get back to work as soon as possible. Cooking was and is so important to me, and I wanted her to see that I was ready, but I could tell I wasn't convincing enough. Professional cooking is fast; it produces results in minutes. I liked that feeling, and I needed the adrenaline rush cooking gave me. For me, the whole process of cooking is flowing and glorious, and while some patience is required, it's not the total package. In those days and up until a few years ago, I found it hard to sit still. Cooking is a constant physical and creative experience that begins and ends in an eight-hour day.

When I returned to work, I felt uneasy. I had no idea what to expect from my co-workers, Gerard and Virgini, or the guest chef, Dittier. Most everyone welcomed me with open arms, but some seemed to be a bit cautious. I figured that was because they didn't know what to say to me. I didn't know what to say to them either, frankly. Let's face

RETURNING TO DAILY LIFE

it, we all felt awkward. When we met the guest chef, he began with assignments for each of us. I was trying to size him up, and what I felt was that he was a seemingly nice guy but really serious about himself. My job that afternoon was to peel whole Granny Smith apples as an accompaniment to a venison dish. I thought I was lucky because peeling apples is usually easy to execute, but it turned out to be a dreadfully excruciating task for me. The circumference of the apple was cumbersome and painful for me to handle.

After peeling a few apples, I couldn't take it anymore and decided to cut them in half, core them, and peel them that way. After a few minutes of doing it this way, the chef walked over to me and asked me what I was doing. I said, "Peeling apples like you asked." His response was to ask you to peel them whole. Then, my first encounter happened with someone. I had to explain the accident to him. I was so embarrassed. I even showed them to him. Without missing a beat, he said, "I'm sorry, but I asked you to peel them whole. Now do it." That seemingly nice guy had just turned into a big, huge jerk. I showed him my hand again and the way I resolved it so it wouldn't be painful, coming up with the same result, but he could have cared less.

As I continued to do it his way, he saw the pain in my face and the tears rolling down my face. "Lisa, if you can't do it right, then go pick thyme leaves. I'll get someone who can peel the apples the right way." Crushed and totally humiliated, I walked to the thyme picking station, and after that moment, I definitely knew I didn't want to go to

France to work under him, even if it meant meeting and learning from Bocuse himself. I realized the importance of understanding technique, but I also knew that each one would have a new way of doing things, and I would honor that. I wasn't going to be as harsh as he was on me. Never! I knew then how important it is to be a team leader, rooting people along, not tearing them down. This was a very valuable lesson.

Many unpleasant, mean-spirited things happened between the accident and twelve years, too many to focus on. If God wanted me to have a thick armor around me, well, this accident certainly made this happen. In retrospect, He wanted me to put the armor of Him over me. I just didn't understand it. After several weeks of reflection, I decided I wasn't going to let my accident hold me back from my dreams. But as I reflect, I was determined not to let the little detail of losing a few fingers get in my way—even though it was a huge detail. I refused to let this adversity make me feel like my life was over, but it certainly took a lot of strength and conscious thought to not continue to self-sabotage myself, but I'm human. There were many to come. At least, I would try my hardest. The days, months, and ultimately, the years following the accident were the hardest of my life.

ME AT SPAGO AT THE FIRST MEALS ON WHEELS
1985

FOR THE LOVE OF GOD & FOOD

8

SPAGO

Fast forward to 1983. I took some time off after leaving L'Orangerie, cooking for Kenny Rogers and other freelance consulting jobs. I'd heard that Ken Frank, another well-known chef in Los Angeles and the owner of La Toque restaurant, was looking for a line cook. It was a temporary job—three months, maybe—but any amount of time spent with any great chef was a plus for my resume, if not for my personal growth. It was my last day at La Toque when Kevin, the chef from "The Good Earth Restaurant" called me as I was driving out of La Toque's parking lot, not knowing where I was going to apply next. I was running of options and was genuinely concerned if word got out about my accident and no one would want to hire me because of this. He told me an opening was coming up at Spago Sunset—a Wolfgang Puck restaurant that every line cook wanted to work at. I asked him how he knew about this, and he said he had his ways.

I hadn't heard from him in six years, and I had no idea how he got my cell number. He said that Kazuto Matsusaka, whom I had worked with at Ma Maison, was leaving Spago to open Chinois on Main, another successful Wolfgang Puck restaurant. I couldn't believe it! Another God wink! It looked like God wanted me to cook. I hadn't seen or spoken with Wolfgang very much since leaving the hospital, so going to Spago unannounced was a little scary for me. I felt a very strange confidence in going, but I wasn't sure how he would react to me, but I was hopeful. Kevin said they were going to need a line cook and that I should drive straight to Spago before word got out. He said to ask for Mark Peel, Wolfgang's head chef at the time. The restaurant was only a mile away from La Toque, so I jammed over in my ridiculously short shorts. It was about ten thirty at night, and the restaurant was still packed. It was such a beautiful place, and it reeked of power you could smell. When I saw Wolfgang, it was like no time had passed between us, thankfully. Seeing him felt like I was home again, and it felt good.

There I was, just four years after working for Wolfgang at Ma Maison, standing at the entrance of Spago and looking right at Wolfgang, who was standing at the bar. Smiling, I told him I'd heard he was looking for a line cook and that he was opening a place called Chinois. Dumbfounded, he asked how I knew, as he had only asked around earlier that day. I told him I'd heard about this from Kevin McKenzie, of whom he didn't know, but that alone should have told me divine intervention was working again. He introduced me to Mark Peel. We shook hands, and as we shook, he looked down, flipping my hand over to see what was missing. I didn't care because Wolfgang was there. I have no idea why that made a difference, but it did. I guess I felt safe around Wolfgang.

SPAGO

Mark said, "So, you want to work here, uh?" Of course, I said yes. Mark was concerned about my speed on the line. Wolfgang giggled a bit as he knew that wasn't going to be a problem. I asked if I could come in and show him one night. I told him my hand had nothing to do with my speed, so a few days later, I came to audition. I was pumped to show Mark my skills and wanted to show Wolfgang how much I'd grown. I was nervous yet confident. I was certain Wolfgang knew I had what it took, and that alone helped me a great deal just to know that. I couldn't believe what my eyes saw that night. Fresh pizzas were made with homemade dough and looked perfect every time, not to mention how delicious they looked and were handcrafted by head pizza chef, Ed La Dou, God rest his soul. He was also the creator of the California Pizza Kitchen's pizzas. The other pizza chef, Serge Falistch, turned out equally amazing pizzas. The Chinese air-dried duck we served was finished in those ovens, too, creating a deep, cherry-caramel color with thin, crispy skin that had a shiny lacquer finish. That duck was by far the best duck in the world—at least, I thought so.

The most popular pizza was the "Jewish Pizza." It wasn't on the menu, but Wolfgang frequently gave it out as an appetizer as a gift to regular customers. It consisted of a perfectly baked pizza crust spread with Crème Fraîche and topped with house-smoked salmon. Then, it was finished with chives and Servuga caviar. Amazing is all I have to say. The sauté station was fun and easy for me, thank goodness. I was responsible for the white butter sauce, which is called Beurre Blanc in French. The base of the sauce is a reduction of white wine, cream, and shallots. Then, you whisk in unsweetened butter on medium to low heat, making a flavorful, creamy sauce. We used it as a base for some of the other sauces. We would add other flavors and reductions, too, and that meant it called for twenty pounds of butter—yikes! I was also responsible for all the vegetable sides, the fabulous veal liver, and sweetbreads—all of them came with sides for these amazing dishes.

***

I started my audition by blanching all the vegetables. This technique stops the cooking immediately and preserves the color of the vegetable. I then trimmed the sweetbreads, the pituitary gland of a cow, which was something new for me and a major pain to clean. But when they are done right—nice and crispy—they are amazing. I prepared the garnishes for all of the dishes and finished the huge vat of Beurre Blanc, which was to be the base for five to six other sauces, and was ready to go—and early, to boot. The anticipation of cooking in an open kitchen in such a famous restaurant also excited me. The evening started and ended faster than any other shift I'd ever worked in my life so far. Not only did I do my job, but I also found myself helping Mark put food on the grill, pulling tickets down for him to put in line for firing, and stoking the mesquite grill

SPAGO

when necessary. Occasionally, when I had time, I would look out into the dining room and see the customers' reactions to the food they were eating.

That was a rush, I have to admit. It felt like we were all putting on a show, and we were. I felt like I'd been working there for years. After it was over, I walked to the back kitchen to put my stuff away. Mark stopped me and said, "Lisa, I have to tell you that you did a great job. I am totally impressed with your speed and organization. You were great. The job is yours." Naturally, I was over the moon with happiness. I wanted to hug him so badly, but instead, I thanked him and told him I couldn't be any happier than I was at that moment. That day was by far the best day of my life. It marked the beginning of my true professional career. My first day at Spago was to be the following Wednesday, so I had about four days to learn the menu. I wanted to be prepared with a few specials, just in case Mark or Wolfgang asked me if I had any ideas. The culinary influence was new and a refreshing change from what was "in" then. Wolfgang broke the mold with California Cuisine, working with flavors from France, Japan, and Italy.

***

FOR THE LOVE OF GOD & FOOD

SPAGO 1986

SPAGO

I had the menu pretty much down and was confident I was ready to go. I wanted Wolfgang to be proud of me, and the confidence I had built since we'd last worked together was in a good place. Deep down, I wanted to eventually be the head chef, so I did my job as well as I could in hopes it might happen someday. The fusion between French and California Cuisine cooking was oddly familiar to me. It felt natural to cook the way he wanted us to. One of the best and most popular dishes on the menu was the boneless half-chicken. It was a super simple and remarkably tasty dish. I'd never seen a chicken filleted like that before. I couldn't wait to learn how to do that. It was stuffed with garlic slivers and Italian parsley leaves under the skin. It was so juicy and clean tasting. Besides the pizzas, the chicken was right up there in sales. The grilled salmon was equally amazing. It was cooked on the mesquite grill on grids that were the thickest and widest I'd ever seen, making it a challenge to cook the fish just right before turning it over. This is when I learned the importance of not turning any protein several times. It causes them to dry out. Turn once, and you are good to go with a juicy piece of fish. I'd never worked with a Mesquite wood grill before, and standing right next to it was as hot as I'd ever felt before. The pizza ovens were right next to the grill, raging at 900 degrees, which didn't help.

The first night was magical. A lot of stars dined at Ma Maison, but I could never see them unless I went into the dining room. But at Spago, I could see everyone and everything because the kitchen was open. Cooking in an open kitchen was amazing, as the energy of the dining room directly affected the energy in the kitchen and vice versa. Barbara Lazaroff, Wolfgang's wife at the time, designed the first exhibition kitchen in the United States for a fine dining establishment. I also couldn't believe I was working at the hottest restaurant in town. Only four short years before, I was somehow meeting some famous people, and from State Beach, no less, while playing volleyball. Wilt Chamberlain was one of the players whom I became great friends with, which led to me being his assistant at all of his wild and crazy parties. I had been a line cook at The Good Earth for a year or so, then at The Great American Food and Beverage Company, then Ma Maison, where my first apprenticeship was, and of course, L'Orangerie. Now, here I was, at Spago. Night after night, I watched Mark expedite and grill food, taking mental notes for when I would be the chef someday. I was more than willing to work hard to get there. I wondered if Mark would ever leave, though. Why would he? I wouldn't. He was in a great position. Watching Ed and Serge, the master pizza chefs, whip out fabulous pizzas was poetry in motion. That was a station I had never worked, as well as pantry and pastry at Spago, too. They all made it look effortless, but for me, it looked insanely difficult.

***

About six months into cooking at Spago, I was promoted to pasta chef when Kazuto left to open Chinois. It was my

SPAGO

own station, meaning I expedited from there and worked in coordination with Mark. If I had to guess, I probably made around two hundred orders of fresh pasta, which was made daily, into yummy pasta dishes five nights a week for over a year and a half. I got very good at cooking fresh pasta and was surprised to find out how difficult it was to cook fresh rather than dried pasta. It cooks faster, and if you overcook it, it turns to glue by the time it gets to the customer's table. Coming up with a special pasta dish every night was challenging but something I loved doing. I was finally asked to start creating my own pasta special every night when one night, Mark and pastry chef Nancy Silverton (and later La Brea Bakery genius and current restauranter) announced they were leaving to get married and start their own restaurant.

I was hoping Wolfgang would choose me as his head chef so badly I could taste it. The night Mark gave his notice, Wolfgang asked all of us in the kitchen to join him for a champagne toast after the shift was over to celebrate Nancy and Mark's future together. While we all toasted their success, I assumed Wolfgang was going to also announce his replacement. My heart was pounding a million miles a minute. I wasn't sure I was qualified to run a restaurant like Spago, but I wanted it to be me, and I knew I could do it. Serge could definitely do the job, and a great one, too. Did I have a shot? Then it happened. Wolfgang said, looking right at me, "I have an announcement to make. Having given this a great amount of thought, I've decided

FOR THE LOVE OF GOD & FOOD

to give Lisa a shot." I nearly fainted, but instead, I cried tears of joy. I put my head in my hands and held back a full-blown cry. I couldn't believe it. Again, God was working His magic, even though I thought it was me. I was going to be Wolfgang's head chef at the hottest restaurant in Los Angeles! I stood up and ran over to Wolfgang, hugging him and kissing him on both cheeks. The feeling I felt at that moment was truly inexplicable.

I expressed my immense gratitude to Wolf, emphasizing how amazed and honored I felt that he had chosen me. I assured him that I would not disappoint him and that I was fully committed to delivering an exceptional performance. In his charming Austrian accent, he playfully remarked that I had better do a good job. While I acknowledged the increased responsibility that came with the task, I had complete confidence in my abilities and knew that I was more than capable of handling it. I relished in the moment. Considering the scope of this announcement, I couldn't help but notice a few faces at the table that seemed filled with disappointment.

It was like I was bathing in the warmest sun and sitting in the brightest moonlight. That was undoubtedly the single most important and phenomenal day of my life, as it brought me to a new level in my craft. I was now part of an elite circle of amazing chefs, accepted and respected by a tremendous community and, most importantly, by Wolfgang Puck. And after all that stress I put myself through over the last few years that I wouldn't be accepted because of a

108

few missing fingers. How could it get any better? Things were blocking up. It was 1985, five years after the accident, and I felt on top of the world—maybe a little too much so. The ego is a delicate thing. It can make us soar, or it can destroy us. My anorexia was out of control more than ever, and unbeknownst to me, I was headed straight for disaster. Well, maybe disaster is a bit strong—but several events I experienced later proved my ego was still in a misguided and lost place.

***

During the two months before Mark left, he trained me on how to do what head chefs do, how to do inventory, how to order food, and in what amounts. Then, there was the importance of food cost, food rotation, the cleanliness of the walk-in, and scheduling. I was to make sure the kitchen manager was doing his or her job as well, and he stressed that I should trust no one. Everyone will want my job, and I should never forget that and trust no one. If I was going to be the head chef of a restaurant of Spago's caliber in the future, that meant I was responsible for everything. So now I was under pressure to be the best I could be. I worked the grill for the last few weeks. Mark was there and learned how to stoke the grill, which was the hardest part of the job. It meant pulling out the heavy grill, which may have weighed easily over a hundred pounds. Adding logs of mesquite wood to the fire was also a challenge, but I dealt with it. The physicality in this kitchen was considerable. Lifting twenty-to-thirty-pound stock pots, sometimes with

FOR THE LOVE OF GOD & FOOD

water or other liquids, was challenging for me. Cases of vegetables to prep my pasta station and other heavy items. Determined to assert my independence, I insisted on lifting and carrying these items myself, as I desired to maintain a sense of self-reliance and autonomy. It was a very big deal back then when women began to emerge in the kitchen to do things like men on many levels, especially the physically difficult ones, but Wolfgang wanted me and other female line cooks to ask a man to do these strenuous things. I thought that was a considerate gesture, but I was in no way going to show any weakness with the male co-workers.

Mike and I had a trip planned in August, way before I knew I was to be a head chef. We had tickets to Kauai for a vacation. Amazing timing, I thought, since Mark was leaving to marry Nancy. I had a feeling I wasn't going to get a whole lot of time off for my actual honeymoon, especially since I was going to take over as head chef, so we decided to use our trip for our honeymoon. I was still friends with my second boyfriend, Terry, and in retrospect, that was pretty cool to me as well. His mother had a cottage on Kauai in Hanalei Bay. Terry invited Mike and me to come join him, his fiancé, his best friend Richard and his wife there for a week. The cottage was right across the street from the bay, and both of us were strong swimmers. I wanted to go for a swim the minute we got there. Hanalei Bay is a relatively large bay, and it looked nice and calm. As soon as we unpacked, we all went to the beach. We jumped into the ocean with enthusiasm and joy, looking forward to

SPAGO

the warmth and beauty of the ocean of Hawaii. We started our swim and immediately found ourselves totally outside the bay within minutes. Mike was way ahead of me, too, which was scary as I realized we were probably caught in a riptide. Frightened, I decided to turn around and swim back to shore. I noticed I was making absolutely no headway and quickly became exhausted. I looked at the shoreline, and it seemed to be miles away from me. Our friends looked like little, tiny dots in the sand. I could faintly see them waving their hands frantically, yelling something at me, but I couldn't hear what they were saying. I looked back and saw Mike swimming towards me. It helped me, but he, too, was trying to tell me something I couldn't hear. I saw somebody on the shore jump in the ocean and could see they were feverishly swimming towards me. Of course, I began to think there might be a shark nearby, so I looked around hysterically for a shark fin, but there wasn't one, and thank God. Exhaustion finally overcame me, and with little strength or desire left in me, I gave in and slowly began to sink to the bottom of the ocean. It didn't seem that far down, as I remember, because I could see to the top of the ocean easily.

As I looked around, I began to feel that same peaceful feeling I'd had in the operating room. Was I going to see the light again? Was I dying again? Was it possible that I still wasn't getting whatever I was supposed to learn in the operating room and from God Himself? Suddenly, I saw an image of a deck of cards playing a sort of movie, flashing my entire life right in front of me. I could even hear it shuffling. I saw my childhood, my teens, my accident, and my entire future being revealed to me. I liked what I saw, especially the future. I don't remember the future the deck of cards showed me, but I knew I had to live, so I forced myself to push off the ocean floor and come up for air. I felt I had a very interesting life ahead of me, and when I popped up out of the water, I released a huge amount of air from my lungs only to find Richard treading water next to me, looking rather relieved I was alive. I was also relieved, to say the least. Richard said we were in a very big riptide and instructed us to swim to the left toward shore.

Before I knew it, and with amazing ease, I might add, we were all on the shore. Still freaking out, I found myself still swimming in the sand and thanking God for yet another chance at life, even though I still didn't believe in God. It is amazing to me that He kept saving me. I was beside myself that I had been given yet more information about my life—and underwater, for goodness' sake, and through a flashing deck of cards. I asked Richard why swim should we swim to the left. He said, swimming parallel to the rip current and the shore to get out of the rip to safety. The week zoomed by, and when we returned from Kauai, I was able to bring my ideas to Wolfgang openly, and he considered some and approved of some. The first dish Wolfgang let me create as a special was a seared sea scallop dish that became a permanent item on the menu. They were served over sautéed spinach with a Frangelico Hazelnut butter

SPAGO

sauce and sprinkled with crushed toasted hazelnuts.

Things with Mike were gliding along at a steady pace, thank goodness, but my main focus was on food and the ever-growing pressures of running a high-powered restaurant. Also, food critics were noticing me, and thank goodness, all the reviews were positive. I was also beginning to notice some jealousy among my peers, which was stressful, but I kept reminding myself of what Mark said, "Everyone will want your job, so trust no one." I was also getting offers from customers to open restaurants soon after becoming head chef. Some were tempting, but I was at the hottest one in town. The "show" from the kitchen was too much fun! The movie stars, heads of studios, writers, directors, and rock stars who came through there were incredible.

People like Mick Jagger and Aretha Franklin, who came in one night very late, I believe it was 12 a.m., wanting dinner. I offered to stay as I wanted to cook for them. Stevie Wonder one night heard his song, "My Cherie Amour," on our sound system and actually stood up at his table to sing along with it! Everyone stopped eating to listen to this incredible man. Gene Kelly was in one night, and as a kid, I thought he was incredible, so the waiter brought him to the counter when I was the pasta chef to introduce me. I was so overtaken with excitement, as we shook hands, my knees buckled! The same thing happened when I met Tom Selleck. Madonna came for dinner just before she became famous. Frank Sinatra had his own chair when he dined at Spago. I could write an entire book about the amazing people that have passed through my life. Swifty Lazar hosted the first Academy Awards Party at Spago. The list of actors was just unbelievable, but I didn't feel nervous about being around them, most of whom I admired in their craft. This was a normal night at Spago and some of the best of my life.

It was time for the wedding. I'm going to condense this experience as it's a long story. The wedding was at a doctor's home in Bel Air that frequented Spago. It had a huge backyard. Ed La Dou made pizzas, and Hana Sushi made sushi. It was perfect. And Nancy made pastries. The day before, I tortured my bridesmaids at the gym by asking them to take niacin, one of my favorite supplements at the time, because I thought it burned fat. It was also tropical weather and rain. On the day of the wedding, the weather cleared, and everything was clean and beautiful, except the wedding parties. I had no idea they were all on cocaine or heroin. The ceremony began, and as I walked down the aisle, I realized I didn't want to marry Mike, but it was too late. But me being not too good at hiding my feelings, they raised their ugly heads in the middle of the ceremony. I said in a very impatient tone, "I do already!" I turned away and walked back down the aisle, but my mom stopped me. She grabbed my arm and, in no uncertain terms, told me to get back up there. Embarrassed, as I had no control over what I just did, I came back to Mike. He had tears running down his cheeks, making me feel horrible. He said let's get through it, and we will deal with it later. What a nightmare.

SPAGO

Then, later, when I didn't think things could get worse, my dad came over to me with tears in his eyes. Thinking he was happy for me, he said, "Lisa, your mother just asked me for a divorce!" I was beside myself, first with shock, then with anger. I had a few words to say to my mom, which weren't nice, but she did something I thought was incredibly selfish and insensitive to not only my dad, but me too! I asked why she couldn't wait until after the reception. Her reply was that my walking away from the altar made her do what she should have done with Dad. No words. Then, the finale happened. When Mike and I got to the Bel Air Hotel for a short honeymoon, Mike jumped in the pool with his Ted Lapidus suit on, confessing later, while drunk, that my behavior at the altar was just too much for him, and thought he'd rather kill himself than live with the shame of it all with our friends and family. I had to jump in to get him off the bottom of the pool. What a disaster. Well, we lasted maybe one and a half years before we divorced.

During the rest of my head chef's post at Spago, which was too short to my own fault, I made a few big mistakes, one of which ended my time there. I finally took an offer to open a restaurant from a regular guest at Spago as it was too good to pass up and made the mistake of sharing this with my newly-hired kitchen manager. I was also going to give a three-month notice before I was to go on vacation to Mexico. This person apparently told Wolfgang I wasn't coming back after my trip, which wasn't the truth. So consequently, when I gave my notice a few days later,

115

he was not happy about it. I think because I took an offer from a client, which is uncool, I broke the golden rule Mark warned me about: trust no one as they would want your job. This was absolutely devastating to me. I absolutely had no idea what to do as there was literally no other chef I wanted to work for but Wolfgang unless it was me. There I was, at the hottest restaurant in LA, if not the world, and then I wasn't because I was too trusting. Now I know (thirty-six years later) it was God. He wanted me to shine on my own, not through another chef's success. But I also know that I could have been with him for a few more years instead of having so much trust in a person.

Mike soon left Spago after this and got a job at Les Anges in Santa Monica Canyon, a premier French restaurant as Maître d'Hotel. One night in 1989, Mike was working, and I decided to go have dinner there. As I drove down San Vicente Boulevard from Brentwood, I turned right on West Channel Road toward the restaurant. As I drove down the road and approached the stoplight, the light changed from red to yellow to green to red in rapid, sequential order. My car stopped running, and the radio shut off without me turning anything off. As I sat in my car, trying to figure out what happened, I tried to restart it to no avail. Then, all of a sudden, and out of nowhere, I noticed a huge aircraft of some kind approaching me from the sky. I closed my eyes for a moment, and when I opened them, I couldn't believe what I saw. It was a massive spaceship, like in the movie Close Encounters of the Third Kind. It was colossal and beyond the brightest white lights I've ever seen hovering over me. It was as if the Coliseum was lit up above me at maximum power. In fact, there is no light on earth that I know of that kind of bright. There was a deep humming sound coming from this humongous beast, and it sounded beautiful. The harmonics reminded me of one of my father's music scores. I remember thinking, There's no way that's what I think it is.

ROGER VERGE & I AT THE BEVERLY HILLS HOTEL

Anxious and full of adrenaline, I got out of the car and stood next to it in the middle of the street. I slowly looked up and marveled at the enormous machine that was suspended over the entire Santa Monica Canyon. That canyon is at least a mile, maybe two miles in diameter, and this ship, or whatever you want to call it, easily stretched over that entire diameter and beyond. Huge, multicolored lights rotated counterclockwise around the outside of this powerful ship. I had no doubt that I was experiencing a phenomenon I had always hoped I would experience in my lifetime: an alien ship. Was I going to get to see an alien, and would it look like the one in Close Encounters of the Third Kind? I felt no fear at all. Feeling full of anticipation and unbelievable excitement, I kneeled on the ground and pleaded, "Please, take me. Please, I want to go with you. I want to learn. I'm not afraid. I can handle it. Please, I'm begging you, whoever you are and wherever you came from, I want to go with you or at least meet you." I was relentless in my asking, and I remember saying that I didn't want to be on Earth anymore. I wonder what motivated me to say that. I did know this wasn't God. The energy was very different. But I felt no threat whatsoever.

***

Did they have something important to tell me? Was there some kind of subliminal information I was to interpret? It didn't feel like it because what I felt in the operating room wasn't this. Something like this doesn't happen to everyone, so naturally, I was feeling special. I also noticed that the lights in the houses in the canyon around me were out. There was only the beautiful humming sound that came from the ship, and it was mesmerizing—hypnotic, really. I continued to stand in the middle of the street, waiting patiently for something else to happen and looking for some type of sign to let me know there might be some kind of life form in there. I wondered if anyone else was experiencing the same thing around me in the canyon. I have no idea how long this event went on, but as I waited for any kind of clue or sign, the stoplight suddenly turned green.

Then, just like that, my car started without me in it while standing next to it, and the radio came back on, playing "Stairway to Heaven" by Led Zeppelin. I remember thinking how bizarre it was that this particular song came on the radio. Then, in almost an instant, the ship lifted up slightly and zoomed off into the sky like a bolt of lightning. As I watched that enormous vessel fly away, I saw smaller ships shoot out around the ship. I wondered if I had been lifted up or transported into the ship and gone to some other planet. Or had I gone anywhere at all? I looked around to see if the lights in the houses had turned on again, and they had not. I got in the car and couldn't wait to tell Mike. Maybe he would think I was nuts. I knew I couldn't call a friend and tell them because I figured no one would believe me. I've always had a vivid imagination, but this was definitely not my imagination. This was the real deal. I felt sad that I experienced this alone.

The following morning, while eating breakfast, I told Mike what happened. As I was telling him this, he was reading an article about a similar event in the paper. It didn't say that there was a sighting, but it said there were several power outages reported in the area that occurred in the canyon that night because of some unknown power surge that lasted for almost twenty-four hours. Mike said, "Wow, that had to be because of what you saw, right?" I was just beside myself. I thought maybe I should call the LA Times and tell them my story. My rational side said no.

I finally received my settlement. So, onwards I went. Where? I had no idea. The next years were very confusing and somewhat lost, but all of that led to something great.

SPAGO

INSIDE BAMBU

FOR THE LOVE OF GOD & FOOD

9
JUMPING AROUND UNTIL IT HAPPENED

I am now wondering what chef I could possibly train under after Wolfgang. I thought of L'Ermitage, but I honestly didn't want to work for anyone else but Wolfgang. I worked for a while at Rebecca's in Venice and West Beach Café. These restaurants were outrageously popular and packed with many famous actors, writers, artists, and musicians. I had many unfortunate experiences with men in the dating world because of my fingers that were very cruel and superficial, to say the least. The stories I could tell, but I won't. I then met my next long-term boyfriend, George, a few months later. We rapidly moved in together after the first year together.

Oddly, Mike worked for the same restaurants, but it was fine as enough time had passed since our divorce. Things went a little weird at Rebecca's with lots of sexual harassment and abuse going on. So, I decided to get out of the business altogether and get a job cooking privately. I got a job in 1987 on "Billionaires Beach" in Malibu for a wonderful couple and stayed there for four years cooking, riding my bike up and down Pacific Coast Highway (without a helmet, I might add), and missing the restaurant business. Then, one day, I heard Wolfgang was opening Granita in

Malibu. George had also left Rebecca's getting a job as a server at Granita. I thought I had nothing to lose, so I called to see if there was any chance of getting a job.

OPENING NIGHT WITH MARC VETRI & ROB 1993

Thankfully, Wolfgang gave me a line cook job. It was way less money, but I thought I'd be his head chef again. But as fate would have it, only six months later, I was approached by Arnold Schwarzenegger to open his restaurant in Santa Monica, California, called Shatzi. I took the position and, I believe, burned that already barely standing bridge with Wolfgang. Excited, I put in my best effort, made a great menu, and within the three months I was there, I was let go for a reason unbeknownst to me. I was crushed. Not only had I probably damaged my relationship with Wolfgang permanently, but I was also out of work again! Depressed, I decided to change careers. I always wanted to be a graphic artist, so I applied to a few schools, and then, God stepped in again! I got a call from the manager of Chaya Venice at the time, a madly popular restaurant and really good too. He knew a man who owned a restaurant in Iceland, of all places, looking for a female chef to bring California cuisine to Reykjavik for four months. God certainly had a plan for me. The good news was that my anorexia was subsiding, and I think a lot of this had to do with the fact that George wasn't having any of my bull. We were also not going on too well, so I thought, What the heck, go to Iceland, Lisa! Travel! Get away from all of it and see what happens!

***

Well, there are no words for the incredible experience I had. Flying into Reykjavik was just magical and terrifying at the same time. It was something like twenty-five below zero and was dumping snow in a wicked blizzard while landing at the airport. I could see the houses below were totally covered in snow as we came out of our descent. We went through a major cloud a mile or two high, and when I saw the runway had no snow, I was totally relieved. I thought we were going to crash! I came to find out that the runway was heated. I was to meet the manager of Amma Lu, the restaurant I was to consult in, as well as The Hard Rock Café. He said I looked Icelandic. It was so cold outside that I thought my nose was going to fall off! The first week I was there, I had a stomachache, mostly from fear of the unknown. My dad talked me through it for a few nights, for which I was grateful. There is so much to talk about this experience, but the most important was how I was beginning to love myself. I was drawing, writing, and journaling. I traveled around this small island in the middle of nowhere, saw Aroura Borealis and so many waterfalls, and marveled at the beautiful horses that roamed everywhere. I also met some amazing people and just lived. I learned how to clean Arctic Char caviar and preserve food. Arctic Char is a cold-water fish in the family Salmonidae, native to alpine lakes, as well as Arctic and sub-arctic coastal waters in the Holarctic. They sit between trout and salmon, leaning more towards trout. It is by far my favorite fish. There were some negative aspects to my trip, but since we are moving in a more positive season, I'll kept it there.

While I was working, George was planning a five-week trip to Europe for us from Santa Monica. He was still working at Granita. And what a marvelous plan he came up with. After my time mostly alone when I wasn't working, I became stronger as a person and a woman. Then a miracle, now I know from God, happened. George called me in Iceland to tell me there was a restaurant in Malibu opening called Bambu. He met the owners one night while waiting on them, Rikki and Jeanette Farr, who asked if he knew a chef who wanted to open a restaurant! He told them about me, and they called and said to contact them when we returned. Jeanette and I had an immediate connection. I felt really good about it and was excited about the opportunity. When George and I saw each other after four months, it was nice but definitely different, at least for me. I had changed. Not necessarily good or bad, but different. We took a plane to Brussels and stayed a few days there and then took a sleeper train over the Swiss Alps all the way down to Rome. There are truly no words to explain what a rush that was. It took a few days on a train track that I have no idea how they built. It was exhilarating and scary at the same time. When we arrived in Rome, I was already missing Iceland.

ME COOKING AWAY AT BAMBU

We did some tourist things, like the Vatican, the Sistine Chapel, and the Colosseum, but the best places were off that path. The food was wonderful, and so were the people. We had a Eurail Pass, so we hopped on the train and went to Florence. Wow, what a city! I could absolutely live there. We rode bikes in the middle of a nasty pollen season, sneezing with the wateriest eyes I've ever had. The pollen was so big it looked like cotton balls.

Then, we were told about the Cinque Terra by a sculptor in Florence, who suggested we get off at Vernazza, that it was the quaintest out of all the other towns along the coast and had the best food in Italy. So, we took off for Vernazza, and when we got off, I was just completely beside myself. It was colorful, as were most of the towns along the Cinque Terra, but this was a special place. Unfortunately, the pastor of the small church in town had just died in a rock-climbing accident, so the town was in mourning. All the restaurants were closed but one. We checked into our hostel, took a nap, and headed down to the restaurant with a huge mosquito bite on my cheek. As we walked, we watched horses pulling barrels of wine on a truck bed. All the people came out and filled their bottles full of red wine that was harvested along the mountainside. We sat down and relished the beauty of this place. I ordered gnocchi that, to this day, never tasted this good anywhere in the world. It was in fresh pesto picked from the gardens all along the Cinque Terra. It literally melted in my mouth. The dessert special was a tiramisu made by a ninety-year-old woman.

JUMPING AROUND UNTIL IT HAPPENED

It was nothing like the American version; this was more like pudding, not a perfectly cut cake. I had the privilege of meeting her and literally begged for the recipe, and she gave it to me! She said it was Italy's peasant dessert. After a few days there, we moved on up to Cannes, where I luckily got to spend the day cooking with Roger Verge's chef at Verge's. We had eaten dinner there the night before and met Roger and told him I was Wolfgang's chef at one time. Then Montmartre, Zermatt, Switzerland and Amsterdam. Amsterdam was like another planet to me. The countryside was just extraordinary as well as the charcuteries and cheeses. But the highlight for me was the Van Gogh Museum. We literally spent eight hours in there looking and re-looking at this brilliant artist's work. By far one of the best experiences of my life. The anorexia had finally faded, and I was eating like a queen. I was hoping I was in alignment for this job at Bambu, too, when we returned. I so needed something amazing to happen to me.

FOR THE LOVE OF GOD & FOOD

10

BAMBU

Upon returning, I met with Jeanette. I was so ready to open a restaurant where I was an executive chef it wasn't even funny. When we met, we immediately hit it off. She had a Jeep; I had a Hyundai and was immediately jealous and made it my mission to get one in the future. We talked and talked, and we immediately knew this was meant to be. Bambu was nestled in a small corner of The Country Mart in Malibu. This space was founded in 1975 by Fred Segal from the iconic clothing store, Fred Segal. He remodeled a run-down motel and turned the apartment complex into small boutiques, including his Fred Segal, in 1980. He was instrumental in bringing fashion retail to Malibu. I've seen many stores come and go in the last thirty years and have also seen a major upgrade in how the storefronts looked. He passed at the age of eighty-seven in 2021. He was quite an amazing man. The interview went so well, she hired me on the spot without tasting any of my food until the night we opened! If that wasn't God, I don't know what is! I could have been the worst cook ever, for all she knew! But lucky for her, I was the best cook ever! I had an idea to create an eclectic cuisine, super healthy and based on food combining. Today, that translates into an organic farm-to-table experience but with some fried/baked beer-battered chicken. I've always yearned to craft unique combinations of French, Asian, Italian, Mexican, and American flavors into my style of cooking, blending these diverse culinary traditions into my recipes. And here it finally was, my opportunity to let my creative go wild!

ME AT BAMBU 1996

Knowing that my customers had a fondness for carbohydrates, I made sure to include them in our menu, since they are essential for our health. I still wanted people to feel great when they ate our food and felt good the next day. I wanted clean, organic, and healthy food, so I made them something I would eat. I was told by my mentor, Wolfgang, to cook what I love to eat, not what I think people want to eat. I never forgot that, so that's what I did. I saw this as my moment to shine and embarked on creating the most exceptional opening menu. I tapped into my creativity like never before, unrestricted by the limitations of a higher-ranking chef. Jeanette, our vibrant and charismatic German hostess, allowed me the freedom to spread my wings. Her maiden's name, "Kuchenmeister," meaning kitchen master in English, perfectly encapsulated her passion for cooking, which she still shares with herself and her friends to this day. Our kitchen, like Spago's, was an open space, inviting guests to witness the magic happening behind the scenes.

We had quite a bit of time to develop the menu and train our staff, also hired floor staff, bar staff, and kitchen staff. I had no idea how I was going to find the kitchen staff, but I put an ad on the Los Angeles Times Craig's List and on in hopes that the best would find me. Well, as it happened, God was definitely involved in this process, even though I had no idea it was Him. I guess my being head chef at Spago helped attract good cooks, but I'd been away from that scene for five years, so I wasn't sure anyone in the business would remember me. But some absolutely amazing people showed up applying for all kinds of positions in the kitchen. Some of the first to apply were hopeful kitchen managers, assistant chefs, line cooks, and then dishwashers. I was

FOR THE LOVE OF GOD & FOOD

going to be cooking and heading the line, not delegating, so I needed two people to be as passionate as I am with food, who cared so much that their passionate energy permeated the food. This is the key to great food. I needed Lisa-time to regroup for the ever-changing ideas I planned on creating weekly. This was of major importance, so God sent these angels to me. I got unbelievably lucky.

The first three people to come to me were just a blessing. Marc Vetri. I had no idea what a gem walked in to be my assistant chef, but I do now! He owns Vetri Cucina in Philadelphia and Las Vegas, Osteria, Pizzeria Vetri, Fiorella Pasta, Alla Spina, Barbuzzo, and Ralph's Italian Restaurant. He has won numerous James Beard awards that cover many facets of his restaurants. He also started Vetri Foundation for Children Lemonade Stand. He bestowed his gifts on Bambu and left in 1996 to go to Italy to learn the best Italian Cuisine, bread, and pasta making. His obsession is his seasonal Panettone bread, and he does it well. In 1998, he opened his restaurant and was one of Food and Wine Magazines Best New Chefs and received the Philadelphia Inquirer's highest restaurant rating! I mean, just wow! I feel lucky to have had him as long as I did. Also, several talented line cooks who ran things for me on Sundays and Mondays were Jennifer, Dave, and Rob. Jennifer was one of the best, as she loved food and had a certain sensual energy she put into her cooking. When she cooked, I knew if I wasn't there, she'd do well. Then Louis walked in. He applied for the kitchen manager, which he got at that moment, as his energy was perfect.

Then there were the almost irreplicable line cooks from Guatemala, Salvador, and Oaxaca. Oh, man, could these guys cook! I would almost always get some dish from them to create specials with. They were all so good and sold out practically in the first hour of opening. The hiring of people was effortless and incredible. God was certainly blessing me. Then, training began, testing recipes and organizing the kitchen. We also had a sushi bar that was probably some of the best sushi in Los Angeles. Go was the sushi master's name. He, too, had innovative and creative ideas I'd not had in a sushi bar before. But, about a week before we opened, I became suddenly terrified of failing, or was it succeeding? Our restaurant was across the Pacific Coast Highway in another shopping center from Wolfgang's Granita Restaurant. I had all kinds of insecurities going on, so much so that I made myself sick.

I literally had a fever that rose and broke multiple times over five days up until opening night. Over the phone, I instructed my staff where to put things, but gratefully, they were all experienced and made it easy for me by inputting their streamlined ideas. I was literally frozen with fear. Then opening night came. I had to get it together and get to the restaurant to make the opening night perfect. Jeanette had spent months, if not over a year, promoting Bambu. Jeanette could see I wasn't feeling well the night we were preparing to open; she gave me, by accident, NyQuil! Within minutes, I was almost not able to stand, so they carried me over to Bernie Safire's Hair Salon, where I passed out. This was at around 3 p.m., and we were opening at 5:30 p.m.! The team provided cold towels for my head and face, along with water, which offered some relief. However, I knew that I had to gather every ounce of strength and determination within me to regain composure. It was quite unusual in the restaurant industry to see an owner like Jeanette working on the sauté station, as it was one of the most challenging stations alongside running the line, which was my responsibility.

FEEDING THE FIREMENT AT BAMBU 1993

So, I got up, showed up, and we all slayed it. We did almost 280 covers that night. Everything went smoothly, and everyone in the kitchen was in total harmony. I was impressed at how Jeanette was so professional and speedy for really never having done line cooking before, plus our chemistry, actually the chemistry of the restaurant staff, was unsurpassed in harmony. We were like an orchestra; every note was perfect. We were a viral hit. To this day, I don't know how I made it through the opening evening, but I do believe now that it was the hand of God. My entire career has been guided by God, without a doubt. I know now that this is what I was born to do.

Since opening night, Bambu was literally packed every night, except in some of the colder months, until it closed on New Year's Eve 1999. We'd become a destination restaurant, which doesn't happen that often. Night after night, we pumped out great food and sushi. Jeanette stayed on the line for about four to five months until she felt the need to go on the floor managing things on a more intimate level. Everyone loved her. She was always making sure everyone was happy and always dressed to the nines. Lots of interesting people, famous bands of the day, and many facets of the movie industry enjoyed our restaurant. I have no idea how our little tucked-away restaurant attracted so many cool people, but I think it had a lot to do with God, Jeanette's tenacious marketing around Malibu, Rikki's involvement with the record business, and word of mouth.

We also received great reviews, which certainly helped.

Among a few "noteworthy" people whom I've longtime friends with since leaving that dined at our humble restaurant were Burt Bacharach, Tony Danza, Rod Stewart, Olivia Newton John (we catered her daughter's wedding), Pierce Brosnan and his wife Keely, (whom I cook privately now and for twenty-two years now who are also great friends), Bette Midler, Don Rickles, Oliver Stone, Robert De Niro, Mel Brooks, Barbra Streisand, Matthew McConaughey, John Paul DeJoria and his wife Eloise, Tony Scott, and his wife Donna, (who I became great friends with, absolutely wonderful people), Tupac, Chris Farley, Robert Downey Jr. to name just a few. Note that I'm not bragging as I could go on and on as to how many interesting people came to our place over the years, from writers to directors, producers to musicians, and many other creative professions. It's about how cool it was. So many artists and interesting people found their way to our restaurant and loved the food and the great energy we put into this magical place. People still remember Bambu like it was yesterday, and it closed almost twenty-four years ago!

When I was introduced to Tony Scott, a remarkable director who has since passed away, and his wife Donna, who would visit our restaurant every week with their dogs and order the extravagant $30.00 cowboy steaks for them, I knew I had to meet these fascinating individuals. Approaching them directly, I jokingly asked, "I had to meet the crazy people who spend so much money on their dogs every week!" This lighthearted comment set the tone for many enjoyable moments we shared at the restaurant, particularly when I initiated Cigar Nights, knowing Tony's passion for cigars. The concept of Cigar Night quickly gained popularity and became a viral success. Every Tuesday, we were packed with want-to-be cigar aficionados, and when we added jazz later on, we could barely accommodate everyone. I was the hostess on this night, with Jennifer leading the kitchen. When Tupac came in the night before he was killed, he sat at the bar, facing the door, looking very nervous, I remember. He ordered a Cuba Libre, aka rum and coke, but he ordered his with Louis the 14th cognac, which runs roughly $4,000.00 for a 750 ml bottle, which means his drink costs around $400.00, and he ordered two that night. We had a small interaction, but I remember him being a gentle person and very friendly, but definitely worried that night. I was saddened the following morning after hearing he had been killed. The night Chris Farley came in, he had the biggest presence I've ever seen, bubbly and friendly. We were packed that night, like every night, and he was partying with some other guys from Saturday Night Live, maybe a little too hard, as he died the next day as well. He was one of my favorite actors. Just like all of our guests, they were normal, fun, and interesting people who happened to be famous. So many talented young people, even more so today, are dying way too young from drugs and alcohol abuse, fentanyl being at the head of the pack.

I have so much to talk about regarding the intricacies of the day-in and day-out of things, the positive and negative, and the very stupid things I continued to do in this very special and difficult environment. In trying to become a better person during this season, I will keep them mostly positive with the inevitable endings and changes that come with growth. I found myself in a more confident, successful, and driven place like I've never felt before. It was my kitchen for the first time in my career. I had total control over the kitchen, with the exception of a few German dishes Jeanette wanted and a peach dessert Rikki wanted. And, in my mind, it was to be the last job I was going to have until I died. I was creating menus like a madwoman, changing the menu almost one to two times a month and inputting them into the computer system myself before prepping.

I wasn't yet close to God, but I was a Buddhist for only one reason: the reincarnation aspect, and I think that was because the idea of coming back seemed easier to live with, as I was terrified of death. But little did I know I would have eternal life with God instead of coming back to do this all over again! I even had an altar that I prayed to. I still didn't understand the concept of talking and praying to someone I couldn't see. Even though that belief wasn't totally fulfilling, I was still fighting to come to God because of that very reason: I couldn't see Him. But I think believing in something else, even though it wasn't God, helped me get through some pretty hard things, but I know now that it was God. Then, several disasters befell us in the next four years that were out of our control, but nothing we couldn't handle. We loved challenges, but these were particularly challenging.

EL NINO, BAMBU AT CROSS CREK MALIBU
COUNTRY MART 1997-1998

FOR THE LOVE OF GOD & FOOD

11
THE MALIBU FIRES AND THE NORTHRIDGE EARTHQUAKE 1993-1994

At the time, I was living in Topanga Canyon, California, with my boyfriend, George. We'd recently relocated from our rent-controlled apartment in Santa Monica to a place at the bottom of Fernwood, just across from the fire station. In February 1993, we also launched our restaurant, Bambu. However, our lives took an unexpected turn when a fire broke out on November 2, 1993. The fire ravaged the coast toward Malibu from Topanga Canyon on Pacific Coast Highway. We were forced to evacuate our home, but George made the courageous decision to stay behind and help fight the fire, despite us not being the homeowners. I crammed our three cats, Elvis, Pricilla, and Dylan, into a crate and jammed down the canyon along with hundreds of others. It was very hot, and I was frightened. Jennifer, our lovely roommate, favorite line cook, and assistant, found a place for us and a few others to stay. Jeanette and Rikki lived in Malibu but were in Lake Tahoe, so they drove as fast as they could to get home, making it back in four hours. Malibu was pretty empty, and when they got to the restaurant, they discovered there was no electricity, but we had gas.

There were thousands of dollars' worth of food in the cooler that would soon go bad, so Jeanette decided to feed the local firemen with the property manager. Most restaurants closed, leaving Bambu pretty much the only one to help feed them. Over a hundred firetrucks from over half the country heard about this, so they parked behind the restaurant in the field where the famous Chili Cook-Off is on Labor Day weekend. Amber, Jeanette's beautiful daughter, recruited them to come to the restaurant to eat. Within hours, there were at least sixty firemen, if not more, from all over the country in line for food we created on the spot, and it grew from there. That was an absolute blast creating whatever we wanted. Some actually would request a dish they saw someone else eating! If we could, we did! Local Malibu residents came to volunteer their time to cook, millionaires and homeless people came to wash dishes, and many gave us money to buy more food from the local markets to feed these amazing men, boys, and women. By the third day, many had come from all over Malibu, offering whatever they could to help. It was a community in full swing, and it felt great. We fed over 4,400 meals to amazing young sweepers from the Dakotas and Montana, women from many states, and veteran firemen from over half this country to fight this fire over a two-week period. Jeanette is a serious go-getter and strong believer in the community, which, in turn, we got to bless these fearless men and women with amazing food. It was a trying time, but I believe God blessed us even more than we already were because of Jeanette's effort and care.

THE MALIBU FIRES AND THE NORTHRIDGE EARTHQUAKE

Then, only a year later, the Northridge Earthquake happened in 1994. That was a horrible one, to put it mildly, at a 6.7 magnitude. I have to say this had to be a 7.6. It was long and violent. But all I can say is I'm so glad we lived in Topanga Canyon, which is a small town near Malibu in the mountains. The night it happened, roughly 4:26 in the morning, we were still living across the fire station on Fernwood, and thank God. We had no water or electricity for a few days, and they graciously let us use their showers. I remember when I walked across the street to ask if we could use their showers, I was talking to a fireman sitting in his truck. Suddenly, there was a big aftershock, in which he insisted I get into the truck for safety. The residents were so polite when waiting in line for water, food, and other provisions. I'd heard of horror stories in more densely populated cities not too far from Topanga Canyon. It was a week or so before we could open the restaurant, as getting trucks and food to the restaurants in Malibu was delayed.

Inspired by the growing popularity of cigar smoking in the nineties, we decided to introduce "Cigar Night" at our restaurant. I thought, Why not dedicate a special evening to this indulgence? To enhance the experience, Jeanette suggested adding a jazz band led by the incredibly talented musician, Chauncy. This addition elevated the already enchanting atmosphere of the evening to new heights. The success of "Cigar Night" was so remarkable that we decided to extend the concept to our Sunday brunch as well, less the cigars. Our Sunday brunch was so incredible.

We had the best eggs Benedictus with a lemony Beurre Blanc. It was much lighter than the classic Hollandaise sauce and was served on grilled sourdough and spinach. Louis, my kitchen manager, made the best-poached eggs in massive amounts. Things couldn't have been better. We were quickly a well-oiled machine. Reservations were encouraged as walk-ins were very high, and what I liked more than anything was how we wouldn't seat anyone who didn't have a reservation if we were totally booked unless there was a no-show or we had a room that subsequently kept a packed bar until there was a table available. Even the President of the United States couldn't be seated if there wasn't a table. Reservations were honored for everyone unless there was a no-show. Taking a table away for a customer who is so-called an 'important person' is a very bad thing to do. Everyone who dined with us was important, and I liked that very much. I was constantly inputting new dishes with the prices into the computer because I was changing it so much that no one wanted to do it. I get bored easily with just about everything, especially with food or feeling too comfortable, because I thought if I was bored, the customers would be, too. I kept the popular dishes like our #1 dish, Chilean Bass, which was cooked on the griddle and served with chopped grilled vegetables, beer-battered onion rings, and balsamic glaze.

There was my Tiramisu, the one the little old lady in Vernazza taught me to make that was so good the Italian restaurant in the same center took theirs off the menu!

THE MALIBU FIRES AND THE NORTHRIDGE EARTHQUAKE

Other dishes included the Lobster Quesadilla, Fried-Baked Buttermilk Beer Batter Chicken, Cowboy Steak, The Lemony Eggless Caesar Salad, Kick Ass Fries, and Eggs Benedictus were among the top best sellers. I created at least three specials a night, sometimes from a fellow cook's idea. Wolfgang was right when he told me to be true to what I like and forget everyone else. Cigar Night was beyond successful. I was able to get Cuban cigars from a dealer and was warned by the FDA if we got caught selling Cuban Cigars, the fine would be upwards of $20,000.00. We didn't care. We just sold them. They were Monte 2 Torpedos, and so good.

I couldn't have been happier. I was floating on a cloud but also on the ground, knowing this time that I was dispensable and had to keep it together. We were at a big party restaurant. I never drank vodka as it was my mother's drink of choice, which she abused but finally got sober later. We drank on the line since the opening and after work. I slowly became a heavy drinker, which wasn't me at all. I rarely drank in my twenties except for Fernet Branca, an Italian digestive I craved. There was a memorable night that will forever be etched in my memory. I was exceptionally intoxicated and never proud of it, either. We always played great music as Rikki, Jeanette's husband, was in the music business. Early on, he put together shows with bands like Rod Stewart, The Beatles, Fleetwood Mac, Yardbirds, The Animals, Pink Floyd, Kinks, Spencer Davis, The Moody Blues, and many others. The song that came on the system was a song by Lynyrd Skynyrd called "Free Bird." The guitar solo is one of my favorites today, besides "Dazed and Confused" by Led Zeppelin. I made everyone stop cooking in the middle of service, jumping up onto the kitchen counter, and playing air guitar! Everyone in the dining room could see me as it was open, and they, in turn, got up from their chairs and danced. Yes, it was nuts, but what a great time our customers had!

Then, if it was possible, we had a major El Nino in 1997–1998, one of the most powerful El Nino Southern Oscillation events in recorded history, resulting in widespread droughts, floods, and other natural disasters across the world. It also caused an estimated 16 percent of the world's reef systems to die and temporarily warmed the air temperature by 2.7 degrees F compared to the usual 0.45 degrees F. It was a nasty rainy season, resulting in a buckled bridge in Malibu that literally cut off anyone coming in from Santa Monica and generally the entire west side. The only way anyone from those areas could get to Bambu or anywhere in Malibu was to take Las Virgenes (aka Malibu Canyon) and Kanan Dume roads from the Ventura 101 freeway.

The water had risen so high in the creek in Serra Retreat that it flooded the Country Mart at Cross Creek Road. It was truly amazing to see the forces of nature at work in such a short period of time. But, to our surprise and gratitude, people made the drive from the westside communities to party with us on Cigar Nights and to eat with us regardless of the inconvenience this put them through. Anyone who knows the 405 and the 101 freeways knows what a feat this is! Bambu was definitely blessed from the start with a supernatural synergy of energy, and I'm quite sure God was at play here. And during those years, I achieved Top 100 Chefs in America three years in a row. This was a big deal for me, to say the least.

In 1998, after the El Nino debacle, came the news of my mom's stage four lung cancer diagnosis at the tender young age of sixty-four. She was given one month to live. She had coughed up a bunch of blood the month before but didn't tell anyone. My dad and mom were divorced for nearly ten years but continued to see each other once a week for dinner, and as unbelievable as this sounds, my dad insisted on adding her to his health insurance just three months before her diagnosis. The story of these two is very sad for me as they were very much in love but going through what most couples go through: midlife crisis changes that sometimes can't sustain a marriage. My mom had an affair in her fifties with her employer at the time. My dad was preparing to leave her when she quit her job and ended it. It was a brief one, but I'm quite sure painful for Dad. He forgave her, which I never thought he would. Then, several years later, my dad had an affair, also in his fifties, with a woman close to my age at the time, who was twenty-eight years old. My mom never forgave him and kicked him out.

My mom and I were best friends, so I told her she wasn't being fair. I told her he had forgiven her, so she needed to forgive him, get some therapy, and move on. But her pride was too much for her to withstand his infidelity. Their entire situation for me was unbearable, as I knew they loved each other. They subsequently got divorced, but still, as a family, we continued to gather together for the holidays. I became very codependent at a very young age, as there was a lot of fighting and unrest in our home, probably because there was no real spiritual foundation in the home. I felt like I needed to try and save the family, but all it did was rob me of a normal childhood. Both parents were big smokers, too, which was obviously why she and my dad got lung cancer. But I also think her bitterness and unwillingness to forgive my dad, whether they stayed together or not, is what gave her cancer. Harboring anger over unresolved anger is detrimental to our immune systems.

When Dad called me to tell me that Mom was dying, it was as though a spear went right through my heart. What was I going to do without her? There were also some amazing memories of her. We had this uncanny way of making each other laugh until we cried on numerous occasions. I could tell her anything, too, and I knew I wasn't going to be given a guilt trip over it. She was only sixty-four years old, but I knew all that anger and unwillingness to forgive was what was killing her, and I told her so. I begged her to forgive him but to no avail. She wasn't going to do any treatment at first, as she said there was nothing to live for since she didn't have Dad (even though she was the one who pushed him away), but she suddenly decided she wanted to live.

THE MALIBU FIRES AND THE NORTHRIDGE EARTHQUAKE

Then, to my complete surprise, my dad broke up with his girlfriend and had her move in with him to take care of her. She endured radiation, which back then wasn't as evolved as treatments today, making her very ill. I never thought my dad had it in him, especially after my mom not forgiving him. Maybe he felt the need to make her see how much he loved her and

hoped she would forgive him. Maybe that was why he did it.

My respect for him went through the roof. He put himself aside for her. I thought that was beautiful. Then, one day, one of Bambu's sushi chefs said he could put her in remission with his special soup with maitake, shitake, and matsutake mushroom broth with burdock root. She drank it daily for a month, and to the doctor's surprise, she went into remission. Thinking she was cured, she stopped the soup, and the treatment ended. Then, one day, a few months later, driving home from work, she called my dad and told him she had a horrendous headache and was going home, but she didn't make it. She had a terrible car crash trying to get off the freeway and was admitted to a hospital nearby downtown Los Angeles. It took Dad two days to find her, and when he did, we all went to the hospital to visit. I was engaged to George at the time. It turned out the cancer had traveled to her brain. She was swollen and in a coma. After a week, she woke up, only to tell me not to marry George because she saw the outcome while in her coma. I was speechless because I was right—others do go to the other

151

side while in a coma. She was proof, and I didn't doubt her because she would never lie to me, especially about something like this. I know she wasn't fond of George, but to lie about this didn't seem like her. I was blown away and decided not to question it and called off the engagement out of respect for her, which was the beginning of the end of that relationship and also, unbeknownst to me, the beginning of the end at Bambu.

She was eventually released back home with Dad. A week before her passing, they had come in for Mother's Day brunch, and I'll never forget the things she said, showing her sense of humor in the face of death. She said that the benefit of having cancer was she could eat all she wanted and lose weight! And when she and Dad were leaving, she looked into my eyes and said, "What am I going to do without that beautiful face?" That was the last thing she said to me. And when my dad passed from lung cancer ten years later, almost to the day of mom's death, he said the exact same thing to me. I knew then that they were going to be together in Heaven, even though I was still not a believer.

On the night of her passing, I was working Cigar Night, which happened to be approximately thirty miles away from my father's house. In the midst of the evening, my father called to inform me that my mother had only about thirty minutes left to live and urged me to come immediately. The previous night, I had bid her farewell, fully aware of the impending tragedy. Before heading to work the following afternoon, I had even played a song I had written for her over the phone, surrounded by friends. We had said our goodbyes, but my father was deeply unsettled by my absence. He believed that I would regret not being by her side in her final moments. However, as someone who is highly visual, I couldn't bear the thought of witnessing her in such a state. The guilt my father tried to impose on me was overwhelming, but I couldn't hold him responsible for it. He had his own unresolved issues with my mother that were separate from my own experiences. I later learned that she struggled emotionally in her last minutes on this earth. As her body transitioned from having cold feet to a feverishly hot head, my father asked if there was anything else she desired. In response, she pointed to her ring finger. Despite their ten years of divorce, my father had never taken off his wedding ring, while my mother had. So, he asked her, "Do you want to get married again?" She nodded her head in agreement.

He took off his ring, put it on her finger, and said, "I marry you; I marry you; I marry you." He then asked her if she could do something for him. She smiled slightly and nodded yes. He asked her to forgive him. She nodded no and passed away! I, to this day, can't believe even at that moment, she couldn't forgive him, which convinces me that her bitterness is what really killed her. This was a defining moment for me to learn with every fragment of my body to forgive, even if you don't get an "I'm sorry" from the person who hurt you. In the months following her death, I dove deeply into the bottle, eventually sending me to what Jeanette wanted for me—a rehab. I refused, so she sent me to a fat farm in Utah for a week to dry out and exercise. It was there I let her go and began healing from this loss that was so painful. I wish I'd been with God then, as I know for a fact that it would have been much easier for me to deal with knowing who she is with now.

DOING DEMO AT EREWHON MARKET FOR OUR BUTTER BARN BUTTER PRODUCTS 2021

Then, at the end of 1998, Paul Newman came in for dinner with his family in December. To make a long story short, he loved my steak sauce and my French Salad

THE MALIBU FIRES AND THE NORTHRIDGE EARTHQUAKE

dressings, so much so he hired me to develop these two items for his company, Newman's Own, and to write two cookbooks for him. I was over the moon with excitement. Not only was I a fan of his movies, but I also thought he was super cool. He was just a normal person, humble and very nice. Then, soon after the New Year started, things at Bambu came to an abrupt halt for me very unexpectedly. I guess God thought it was time to move on. Let's just put it that way. But at the time, my major dreams of being there until I died were shattered beyond my expectations. I had done nothing to cause this (at least I was unaware of), but it happened.

I spent a good five months very sad and depressed over this. But I had a new job, and I had to get to work. George was still working at Bambu but didn't stay long after I left Bambu. Things slowly started to fall apart for us, and about a year after Mom's death, I moved out. I moved in with a friend, one of our hostesses, to Calabasas, California, where she lived while going to Pepperdine University. George and I were together for eleven years and had a wonderful time together, but it had run its course, but it still didn't make it any less painful to move out. I don't know about you, but there were a lot of changes in a very short period of time. How I got through it all was because God was by my side, I didn't know that at the time, but I certainly was being covered in His strength and love.

FOR THE LOVE OF GOD & FOOD

Frank and I on our Wedding Day 2016

12

AFTER BAMBU

So, in 1999, yet another journey of healing began, and almost immediately. I had no time to really be upset because my new job started a few weeks after being let go, which in itself was a blessing. The next two years changed drastically for me. Getting over not working at night was the hardest part, both physically and psychologically. My sleep schedule was a mess, causing me to feel depressed and restless. Sitting more than I ever had in my life to write was so foreign to me. So, I began writing the cookbooks Newman's Own Cookbook and The Hole in the Wall Gang—A Children's Cookbook.

I also learned about how recipes are made for the masses, and it was nothing like I expected it to be. I was to make only a two two-quart recipe for each item that would be input into a computer to make 250,000 bottles! I was amazed! They were called Newman's Own Steak Sauce and Newman's Own Parisian Salad Dressing, which are no longer available. Before I knew it, I saw them on the shelves of big markets like Vons, Albertsons, Gelsons, and so on. I couldn't believe that I had developed these and the masses were buying them. This was a very big deal, and it also freed me up to start a catering business. I had no idea how I was going to get customers, but God once again had another plan for me.

When my job was done with Newman's Own in 2001, I needed to find another job, and I did pretty soon after. Actually, it found me (as it always has my entire career) for an old State Beach friend who owned a restaurant in West Los Angeles called Hana Sushi was opening another Hana Sushi in Sun Valley, Idaho. I was so thrilled to be getting out of Los Angeles for a while and was hoping to make a fresh start there. Maybe even moving there. I'd heard it was gorgeous, a small town, and had great skiing. I hadn't skied in a very long time, but I was in pretty great shape and looked forward to revisiting this fabulous sport. I spent several months developing the menu until I finally went up there to survey the restaurant space and see how the open kitchen should be designed. I was also starting to get catering jobs until it was time to go and open the restaurant. This was quite the experience and very short-lived. When I arrived, the lodging that was promised to me was occupied, which made me feel uncomfortable. But within minutes, he asked the occupant to leave. I also recruited a bartender/ server from another restaurant to come help us open it. I felt like a kid, but what I was experiencing was a midlife crisis.

The owner had misled us into thinking we were going to open before Thanksgiving, but that wasn't possible as he had at least two to three months of construction yet to be done. So, all of the employees that had come there to work, including me, spent two months cementing black stones he brought in from Mexico on the walls. Since there wasn't much to do in the kitchen yet, I decided to learn to snowboard. Never in my life did I think I would want to learn how to snowboard, as I was forty-four years old and a skier, but it looked like way more fun without the poles! I became addicted and spent just about every morning snowboarding before the shift at the restaurant. That alone was worth the trip to Sun Valley, which, as they said, was gorgeous. I made new friends and connected with the old ones who lived there. I was already planning to permanently move there. The magic of Bald Mountain and Dollar Mountain, where I learned to snowboard, was so strong that I found myself willing to leave behind my family and friends. The serene beauty and majestic presence of the mountains had a profound impact on my well-being, both physically and spiritually. I felt a sense renewal like nowhere else I'd been. The mountains became a sanctuary, a place where I could find solace, clarity, and a deep connection to nature. Then, the opening day was upon us, and what an opening it was. It was uncannily similar to Bambu. Everything about it. We had my eclectic cuisine in an open kitchen and also a sushi bar. Stars packed the place as well. Then something unfortunate happened.

One day, and without any warning or idea that something as unimportant (at least to me) was to change the course of my life in the way I wanted it to, I was framed yet again, and I must say in a very clever but malicious way. But, unbeknownst to me, in fact, I was again being saved and protected by God. One of the sushi chefs gave me day-old blue fin tuna (something they never use as raw sushi the next day) to make for the staff meal. I asked him three times if he was sure about that, and he said yes. They almost always use it as a giveaway when you sit down, marinated in soy or something that "cooks" the fish. So, I went ahead and made a nice dinner for everyone. When the sushi master came in after his break and heard about this, he shoved me up against the dishwasher, yelling at me and trying to choke me for using that tuna. I went into full self-defense mode. Never have I even known I had the kind of strength I had at that moment. I managed to kick him in the crotch with my knee, bolted out of there like a rocket, and told the owner I quit.

Devastated, I ran to my apartment, which was a few blocks away, packed my stuff, and left. I cried the entire way home. I was literally planning the rest of my life in Sun Valley. I found out later that the cocaine use there was rampant. No wonder the sushi chef and the owner were psychos, and because of that reason, the restaurant started to fail, causing the owner to sledgehammer the walls to pieces and take everything he could in a truck in the middle of the night and was never seen again. I'm telling you, the restaurant business is not for everyone!

When I rolled back into Calabasas, I told no one,

not even my roommate Alaina, that I was coming. But God stepped in yet again! I got a call from my old sous-chef Jennifer telling me that Keely Brosnan, Pierce Brosnan's wife, was writing a gardening cookbook with recipes and was looking for chefs to contribute. I got the interview, and she hired me to help and also cook for small dinner parties. This was also in late 2001. I also got a personal assistant job in Studio City. I was feeling so lost about what I was going to do for the rest of my life. But as time went on, I began to get more and more catering jobs. Honestly, I don't remember how, as the internet was not really a thing yet, but word of mouth was slowly growing. I am still cooking for them today, twenty-two years later.

Then, in 2005, I reconnected with Frank, who was a regular customer at Bambu and was there on opening night. Over the five years I was at Bambu, we would run into each other either at the restaurant or elsewhere. He was and still is very handsome, and I liked him. Then, as fate would have it, I was catering on Easter Sunday 2005 for my friend, and Frank was there. We sat next to each other at the table. After dinner, I had to leave as I had a date with an old high school friend and had to leave, but Frank wasn't having it. He put his hand on my leg and said, "Cancel it." That was it, and here we are, eighteen and a half years later! I had no clue he was interested in me, but then again, I never thought anyone was interested in me!

Then I landed a job at a famous rehab in Malibu in 2005, right about the time Frank and I started dating seriously, which was within a four-month period until he moved in. We never talked about it at all until I came home one day. He was building a chest of drawers in my bedroom! I'm like, "Are you moving in?" He answered, "Yes, is that a problem?"

I really didn't know how to respond to this, so he moved in. We are definitely not your conventional couple by a mile. It was a small rehab that went from nine clients and soon blossomed into a hundred clients over the next three years as they owned the entire block of houses for different types of treatment. I was running a restaurant! Working in this environment was absolutely toxic. I didn't realize this until I was gone. The disfunction was just unbelievable. The ones with eating disorders couldn't fool me as I was a recovered anorexic! I was actually their therapist as far as they were concerned, telling me things they didn't tell their actual therapists. I, of course, in an effort to help them, would share these conversations with them. The people that came through had money as they didn't take insurance. I had one very famous person give me the menu the chef on their yacht would prepare for breakfast, lunch, and dinner. They were there recovering from plastic surgery, so maybe they weren't aware of what they were giving me because of pain meds. In every dish and every meal, there was vodka! It was in the salad dressings, the protein shakes, the soups, the sauces, and desserts! The stories I could tell. I actually prayed for them but was not yet with God. I felt horrible for them because any addiction is like being in prison. It's just awful.

Then, in 2008, I applied for Top Chef. I came super close to getting on the first season, but it wasn't meant to be. Then I auditioned for "Hell's Kitchen" and didn't get on that one either, as I think I was a bit too feisty. Then another show called "The Chopping Block" found me as they saw my audition for "Hell's Kitchen," and as luck would have it, the producers recognized me and said it was the funniest audition they'd ever seen, so I got on the show and with my ex-husband to boot. It was a couples show of all kinds, mother-daughter, sisters, husbands and wives, etc. These were, by far, some of the best times I've had! I even got engaged to Frank when I came home! Then, a miracle happened. I got a call from someone soon after returning who found me on Yelp.

I was hired to cater a pre-Emmy event at a private residence in Malibu. After that, a few weeks later, they called me again to see if I knew anyone who wanted a four-day-a-week job cooking. I was like, "What about me?" They went for it, and that lasted until 2017. I was also planning my wedding with Frank, and my employer graciously offered his beautiful home in Malibu for our celebration.

Frank and I started our wholesale baking company in

2016 called Butter Barn Butter. It started as a flavored grass-fed butter company and morphed into a gluten-free, all-organic, non-GMO cookie and brownie company, with some vegan products, too. If you remember my Paul Newman experience, God was planting the seed for me to start my own company. Frank and I were married in September of 2016, which was as magical as I could have imagined it to be. The rental company I used for catering gifted the rentals as a thank-you for using them over the last fifteen years, and the gifting on our special day didn't stop there. So much love was everywhere!

I love God. He always knows what's best for us even if we don't, and even if it's painful, full of loss and failures. But I now know—there are no failures. Without those, we wouldn't know success. I also know that when God has a purpose for us in this life, the enemy is always hard at work trying to sabotage it. That's when life gets difficult, and you know you're on the right path.

13

THE YEAR I CHANGED

Although it took me many more years to find God and myself, my faith and understanding of genuine forgiveness, I plugged along anyway down many paths. I actually had to work at it. My spiritual "house" was empty. I lacked any real understanding of how much I needed to believe in something other than myself. I did have spirituality, but it wasn't strong enough for me because it was based on my way of doing things. For me, this way of living didn't quite hit home for me anymore, especially since I found myself tempted in my old ways from time to time. I wanted a permanent solution. Relying on myself for decision-making and knowing it all clearly brought me problems and dissatisfaction. I wanted to feel clean, and no number of showers could clean up my mess. I knew I needed to move forward in my spiritual house but had no idea where to start or how to do it. So, the journey began, and it started with Louise Hay. Her affirmations and positive thinking had healed many from deadly diseases, so I decided to try and recite Louise Hays's affirmations in hopes I would grow spiritually and change the way I thought about myself.

I was still suffering from low self-esteem up until 2011, but I was feeling better about my body than ever before. I worked hard at believing in the words I was "reciting." Even though I kind of didn't understand how changing my negative thought process would "cure" me, I continued to recite them, anyway. But to my surprise, her methods did work, and I experienced their power when using them for anorexia. What I did like about how Ms. Hay is how she saw things was how she spelled disease as "dis-ease." If you really think about that spelling, I was in a state of dis-ease within my body, soul, and mind. But at the time, it was the best I could do to continue writing these reaffirmations on post-it notes and placing them all around the house, mostly on my bathroom mirror. It was the first thing I would see every morning, yet I managed to ignore them often. It was hard to read them out loud. It meant I had to change and create acceptance, and I wasn't ready for that, but I plugged along. It was like I thought I could rub a lamp, and some genie would pop out and heal me in an instant. I wanted immediate results in every part of my life. I knew I didn't want to have to go through the pain of soul-searching, but it was inevitable if I was going to change. What matters most is finding meaning and fulfillment in the things we are passionate about, and for me, that was creativity. Rather than seeking validation or approval from others (which I constantly did), it more than likely resulted in sabotaging my own success. Ultimately, it is up to each individual to determine what is worth their time, effort, and attention. After a while, I gave up reciting affirmations and kept wandering in and out of the light and the darkness. I'd put on ten pounds, which felt like fifty pounds for me, which took a while to get used to. As much as she helped me, for which I will feel forever grateful, I wasn't feeling my heart or soul at the deepest level for me—the places that were truly at the root of my dis-eases and lack of self-confidence. Logically, they made sense to me, but there was still no real commitment for me. I needed something much bigger than what I recited to heal—even though that did help. I needed that experience in the operating room. I wanted a real core connection with something that felt right and natural.

***

I was still rough around the edges. I even had an altar with all types of Buddhas and other idols and hoped that having all that "stuff" in an organized fashion on a table would magically change my life and save me from having to go through all the agony of seeing who I really was. So many words have come out of my mouth that I wish I hadn't. All the swearing I did and the nasty things I said to people were ridiculous. It got so bad that an old friend gave me a coffee-table book called The "F" Word. For some reason, when I got that book, it suddenly made me feel embarrassed. I felt like a joke. It wasn't so funny anymore that I swore incessantly, so I threw it away. To this day, I wonder what people thought was so funny about my truck driver's mouth. People never forget the words we say to each other. That old saying, "Sticks and stones may break my bones, but words will never hurt me," is a bunch of nonsense, too. I have pretended that words never hurt me, but they have, and deeply. Not to mention the words I've used to hurt people. But how could they have known if I didn't say something? Ultimately, I knew that if I came to God, that would mean admitting all of the wrongs I had done in my life, and I didn't want to admit them to anyone, especially God! It would be too difficult to look at myself that intensely and honestly. But still, it wasn't enough. So, I learned how to throw tarot cards in the aftermath of a horrible and heartbreaking breakup with a married man, no less. That's a whole other story I won't share here.

There I was again, trying to find answers and thinking I could get them by throwing a deck of cards. I spent countless thousands of dollars on psychics. I don't want to think how much, really. It's embarrassing to even admit it out loud. I was so lost. I mean, I wouldn't doubt that they had a post-it by the telephone at The Psychic Eye Bookstore in Sherman Oaks that read, "Lisa Stalvey, the huge sucker that will believe anything we tell her."

As I reflect back on all of the incredibly thoughtless things I've done to myself and others and how many I've hurt, I am also grateful to have persevered in my journey to become a better person. Further, I now know I needed to go through all of it to come to where I am today, which has given me major comfort. To name a few blessings: Not everyone gets to be Wolfgang Puck's head chef at the hottest place in town, and as a woman, to boot. Not everyone gets to meet Paul Newman, co-write two cookbooks, and develop two products for his company. Not everyone gets to develop spices for a meat company that has one on the shelf today. Not everyone gets to live a life doing what she truly loves to do in life. My talent as a chef is truly a gift from God.

After the passing of my mother, I found myself deeply intrigued by the metaphysical aspects of illness and disease. It felt like a divine "download" from God, tailored specifically to address my long-standing fear of sickness, which still lingers within me. Throughout my life, I have consistently reaffirmed my disbelief in the existence of flu, cancer, and other diseases. I perceive them as products of the modern programming of the twenty-first century, perpetuated by commercials and subliminal messages aimed at generating profit. The notion of flu season and the pressure to get vaccinated for protection has never resonated with me. Even during the pandemic of 2020–2023, when society urged us to isolate ourselves and restrict our activities, I held firm in my belief that we possess incredible healing capabilities within us. We simply need to prioritize our gut health, maintain inner peace, and listen to our logical instincts. These principles were instilled in me by my father during my childhood. Our household never contained processed foods; everything was organic and carefully chosen. Now, I continue to prioritize my well-being, hoping to lead a long and healthy life. As I delved deeper into the understanding of disease, I began to recognize the profound connection between emotional, physical, and spiritual well-being and its impact on our overall health.

I also believe arguments between people who love each other are usually about the individual's place on their path. When they don't align is when we argue. No two people grow at the same time, so we must be loving and patient with each other until we catch up. I thought love was like this because of how horrible Mom and Dad fought, especially right before the divorce. I thought this was "normal"! I had thought I had improved in that area, but I hadn't. This, I believe, is where the residual and unresolved events in past relationships and family traumas we never deal with will come up, bringing those issues into the next and the next and the next relationships and workplace. I wanted peace in my life, and I finally realized it was I who had to change. It was time to do something serious. Finding work had also become hard. I'd never had a hard time with that, but when the recession hit in 2007, I did.

I thought I would never have problems getting work with my resume. Maybe I was too experienced, and that's why I couldn't find anything. Plus, saying there wasn't any work to be had, at least, that's what I told myself. I constantly reaffirmed there was no work. I literally talked myself out of a job. But my attitude of fear, negativity, gloom, and doom I was feeling during that time was scary. I was terrified at the thought of being homeless, even though Frank would have taken care of what I couldn't handle. I was and still am fiercely independent, and the idea of needing his help wasn't an option and still isn't. I got work occasionally, but not enough to make ends meet, which made me terrified. I wasn't used to a man taking care of me on any level. I needed emotional support more than anything else. It made me feel weak to need anything, and having no Faith at all made everything, I'm sure, much worse. It is inevitable that feelings of love, happiness, and joy have a profound impact on us, whether we like it or not. Often, we remain unaware of the consequences when we fail to address these emotions. However, once we awaken to their presence, we are faced with the task of reconciling the hurtful words we have spoken to others and forgiving those who have hurt us with their own words. This process can be a journey we take alone, but it is crucial for our happiness and well-being. Personally, I have found solace and guidance in turning to God as one of the ways to navigate through these important issues. During this season, I spent countless hours sleeping and living in fear when I was awake—which I know now kept me from getting work in the first place. How could anything positive happen to me while I was in that state of mind? Who would want to be around that, especially if I'm cooking their food? Not me.

FOR THE LOVE OF GOD & FOOD

***

During my lowest point, I confided in my Christian friends about my spiritual rock bottom. They suggested that I visit the Pasadena International House of Prayer, assuring me that it was not a typical church setting but a place where people would pray for me. They understood my skepticism and emphasized that I wouldn't be pressured to make any immediate decisions. Although I wasn't particularly enthusiastic about the idea, I thought to myself, Why not? What harm could it do? After all, nothing else seemed to be working. Uttering the words "prayer," "God," and especially "Jesus" didn't come easily to me, but I felt a calling toward it. It seemed as though God knew I was finally ready to act. I felt if I didn't take some kind of action soon, I feared I would lose the man I truly loved and wanted to spend the rest of my life with only because of my lack of joy, happiness, and love. The urgency of the situation was unlike anything I had experienced before. Above all, I knew deep within my soul that I needed a miracle. Thirty-one years of enduring this struggle had been enough.

***

As I walked in the church, two lovely women greeted me. They touched my shoulder, and I felt like what I thought I knew and was in control of didn't exist anymore in me. It was bizarre. I can't explain it, just like in the operating room. The lightness I was so desperately searching for since that day in the operating room was finally alive.

THE YEAR I CHANGED

Bodybuilding, anorexia, and wanting to look perfect were not the answer. Where real happiness lies is in our souls. I felt a kind of cleansing come over me, and all that "dirtiness" I'd felt earlier in my life seemed to be healed just like that. I felt as though everything I had done before that was bad was forgiven. I like to describe my experience with these women at that moment as a "humbling place of hope." What I experienced was nothing short of a miracle.

My heart was filled up with love within seconds, almost as good as my encounter with God. It was healing on the soul level, something not found in this world. No one was pressuring me to convert, either. They were just there to help me. Their actions alone were proof for me because of the genuine love they showed toward me. They asked why I was there, and I told them for help. I was exhausted and tired of trying so hard to please people just so they'd like me, and I was tired of my pride and ego, which resulted in fighting a lot. I mean, there's a healthy need to want people to like us, but to what extent? It took me a while to understand that attempting to please people was futile and not important. There is emptiness to that kind of existence, but it kept me busy and away from my own problems.

***

As they talked and prayed over me, I felt the same warm breeze I felt in the operating room. God was there with me, too. The way they were talking was in a way I'd never heard anything explained to me before. There was no judgment in how they were helping me. They said that God was pleased with me and had been my whole life. Really? I was a reckless person and a non-believer for my whole life. Then I began to see that I was, in fact, at that moment, being released from my pain, and I found myself completely free. I cried tears of release, joy, and hope. I was intrigued by the idea that I could trust something I couldn't see because He lived in me. This is what they meant by faith. As scary and weird as it sounded to live life in faith, it's the only idea that has softened my heart and calmed me down over the past twelve years. I am a totally different person today. My friends noticed a major change in me, too. Some wanted what I had, some were uncomfortable with what I'd become, and some, mostly my Jewish friends, wanted to know why I believed in Jesus. I asked them why they didn't! After all, Jesus was Jewish and a Rabbi! Frank said he had been waiting for me to come to God and Jesus for a long time. Nothing I tried before influenced me like that, and I wasn't trying. The awareness they were showing me in myself began to emerge.

After listening to these two women talk for a time, I told them about my experience in the operating room and asked how one let go and let God. One of the women said it was simple. It means to live totally in the present, living minute to minute, not thinking about the past or the future, and knowing God is there with you. Just know that there's a plan for you, and all the planning and worrying you do won't change what will happen. We all have a destiny.

Some come sooner than later. I sort of got it, but I also didn't get it. They asked what I did for a living, and when I told them, they asked if this was what I wanted to do in life. I said I wanted to be a fashion photographer. They asked me why I thought this didn't happen. I said I thought it was probably very difficult to break into. They asked if I'd ever once found that cooking was a hard profession to break into. Honestly, I'd never thought about it. It just happened. They asked if I knew why, and I guessed it was because it was effortless, like all the signs on my road pointed to cooking even though I wasn't looking. I agreed but said I went through a lot of pain and hard work. It definitely hasn't been a cakewalk. She said, "Of course, it hasn't been easy, but your accident made you think things had become more difficult, and many of your dreams associated with cooking ended for you. Yet, the ease with which the opportunities showed themselves to you and how you couldn't explain to anyone why you were so gifted in many areas of your profession seemed odd to you, didn't they?"

I was blown away had how her words shifted the way I'd been thinking my entire life about things. I wanted to shift my thoughts and words to positive ones instead of negative ones. That's what "letting go and letting God" means! In a word, it's Faith. You naturally followed the path that was given to you without questioning or ever understanding why. I was just blown away. I tried to leave my career several times, but God brought me back every time. That door never closed, even through all the joys and hardships I faced. She went on to say that the more I pursue God and talk to Him daily about my hopes, dreams, things I want to change, an addiction I want to be healed from, I will see my life transform in every way. You will see a more loving, free-from-opposition relationship in no time if you are diligent and consistent in your own growth with God. Be the example. Unfortunately, we learn many bad things when we are young that need God's healing. Look for the signs, pray before bed, and you will have answers in your dreams.

Those beautiful women showed me a different perspective of life that day, and everything I've gone through had to happen, and that I had been given a gift and never once asked myself why. I realized at that moment that I chose to torture myself because I couldn't understand why everything was so easy for me. I actually felt guilty about that. I was on my path, my gift from God. I knew and saw so many around me my whole life struggling with what they wanted to do with their lives or what their purpose was. I could see what their God-given talents were, even though they couldn't, and I tried to encourage them to pursue what they love. Wondering what our purpose in life is can be very frustrating and scary. She said that God has more for me and is ongoing until He calls me home. All of what you've gone through is preparing you for what's to come. I liked that a lot.

I asked, "Really? Do you know what that plan is?" There it was again, wanting to know before something happened! Of course, she said no, and it was not for her or me to know. You

THE YEAR I CHANGED

just have to let it all go and let God. Have faith and trust Him entirely. Thank Him daily, as many times a day as you need, for providing for you, for loving you, for being there for you, for healing you, and whatever else you want to thank Him for. That's all. And don't be afraid to talk to Him just like you would your best friend or even us. Everyone these days makes a big deal out of how we are supposed to pray. There are no rules. He's next to you all the time. I've never prayed before, but I like the idea of just talking to Him like a normal person. I liked that idea a lot, but I knew it would take me a while to understand the power of prayer and how it would feel to trust and let it all go to something I couldn't see. Faith and trust have been two difficult things for me to comprehend throughout my life. I had been burned so many times, some of it of my own doing and others just being jealous or mean-spirited. Over time, I decided to test the idea of living just one whole day in faith, and when I noticed how powerful it was to live like that, I began to do it more often. Now I do it all the time. I thank Him constantly. Over time, I began to notice the blessings I was receiving, but all along, He had been giving me blessings even while I didn't believe. He is so forgiving. Talking to God was working in my life, and better than I could have ever imagined it to be. There it was—the true messengers I'd been seeking my whole adult life, and I found them in a small church in Pasadena and not at The Psychic Eye bookstore in Sherman Oaks. That day, I met God, and my life hasn't been the same since.

FOR THE LOVE OF GOD & FOOD

14

COMING TO JESUS

It took about a year after that day for me to fully understand the extent of who Jesus is. I was actually still embarrassed to say His name. I shared my experience with my friends, and they were elated. One of them bought me a Bible and daily prayer books. My life has changed greatly in the last few years and for the better. I noticed as I started speaking freely about my newfound beliefs with Frank, and he was very happy to hear it, but some weren't as open to this newfound happiness for me as I thought they might be. That was a bit surprising, but then again, not really. I guess I shouldn't have been because I didn't welcome this belief until I was fifty-four years old. I mean, it's not like I'm walking around asking people if they've found Jesus. I don't bring up my beliefs with my friends unless the conversation lends its hand to talking about God.

Many have noticed a certain "glow," "light," "energy," or "transformation" in me. When they ask me what I've done, I tell them the truth. I'm not afraid to share my Faith, not one bit. I also add that I eat well and organic and that I don't (and really never have) believe in "disease," cancer, the flu, etc., and of course, they think I'm crazy. They then ask me why, and I tell them I've found God, and all of my worries and fears are in His hands now;

I trust Him implicitly to take care of me on every level, including financially. Some argue with me, some blow over it, and some want to know more. I ask Him to show me the way every morning and if needed and all day long. It's a relationship with God, not a religion.

And the closer I get to God, I am walking and will continue to walk on what seems to be an ever-narrowing path in life, and that's okay. At least I'm at peace. I am working on being a better person. I am now happily married to the man I used to argue with and am enjoying a much more peaceful life with him. God answered my prayers. All I know is this: I love God and how I've been feeling since finding Him. No one can keep me from feeling this way and from sharing how God has changed me. I want others to feel like I do and feel that it is my responsibility to share. I used to get angry when people talked to me about God and Jesus, too, so I don't judge anymore. This is God's job, not mine. I was threatened because I had no idea what they were talking about, and placing my entire life into the hands of someone or something I couldn't see was insane to me then. Now, I can't live in this world anymore without Faith, and honestly, in this time of civilization, 2023 to be exact, I don't know how anyone can live without Faith, God, or Jesus and feel safe. I'm of this Earth, not in it. I struggled somewhat with needing people in my life to feed me drama during this transformation, but He literally removed them from my life—and effortlessly, as if they vanished into thin air—I now see why. And honestly, that wasn't easy either.

COMING TO JESUS

Some were friends for over twenty years and were people I would never have guessed would leave. But I guess it's part of the big picture and His plan for me. I have much more to accomplish. I know that now, and I can't wait to see what unfolds. I miss them dearly, and how long they will be absent, only God knows. I accept and totally trust Him and wherever He chooses to take from me or bless me. I know now when a door closes, a better one will open. Actually, it's a very exciting and peaceful way to live!

***

I understand now that my experience with God in the operating room was necessary and a blessing, but I was too unaware of what a gift that was. I obviously couldn't handle the message He gave to me there at that time. We are fragile souls, and we live within such a stream of unconsciousness that to realize the Mightiness of God within us in an instant would be virtually impossible to withstand. Change like I experienced that day at the Pasadena International House of Prayer couldn't have happened overnight or at any other time. It was perfect. Looking back, I now realize that all the different roads I had to take over the last thirty-one years were absolutely necessary for me to grow. Every nuance, heartbreak, pain, sadness, disappointment, the loss of my babies and my fingers, and all the painful circumstances I experienced were totally necessary for me to get where I am today. Some people would look at these experiences in life as punishment from God. When people tell me something tragic that happened to them and blame it on God, I quickly tell them God wouldn't do that. Only the enemy would do that. Evil in this world is not driven by God. The enemy has dominion over this Earth, and especially in these times, it seems the worst. This tells me Jesus is returning sooner than we think.

The key is to be patiently impatient, which is almost impossible. Waiting for our illumination becomes lost in our daily need for survival. I never saw this or could have ever understood this, and I feel sad that I missed many days of my life by being impatient. Better late than never. Always looking at the future and the past and never living in the present, I know now was, in fact, what caused my emptiness. I also know now that no matter how dark my past has been, it has now been erased, and just like that. I feel like a child, full of innocence and clarity. The fire was lit under me that very afternoon, and it will never go out again. As I come closer to living with God, the darkness tries to creep in often as the enemy loathes joy and happiness. I know that Frank was meant for me now more than ever. The pain we both were working out from our past relationships and painful childhoods nearly destroyed us, but we hung in there out of pure love with no option of breaking up.

And when I came to God, I fought for us with a vengeance, determined to live how God intended us to

COMING TO JESUS

live, covering myself and us in the Blood of Jesus and the Armor of God. That no weapon formed against would prosper. I am free from the chains of unhappiness, jealousy, anger, and the need to impress others. I still have the choice of free will, as we all do, and I hope I am making better decisions, but it feels better to leave everything to God now. If it weren't for my accident, I might have found myself in much darker places than I ended up in. It could have been much worse, so much so I can't think about it. It's gone now, all that pain, and now I look forward to each day and thank God for it. I look back at who I was, and I can't believe it. I live each day now as if I were flowing down a river in a boat. I have two choices: hit the big rock in the middle or go around it. Too often, we make life more difficult on ourselves than we need to, but then again, we are human.

***

In closing, I was baptized again in 2013 at Calvary Church in front of hundreds of people, sharing how God released me from my dis-eases. It was an amazing feeling. I have no idea what the future holds for me now, and I love that. Only He knows my last day here on Earth and what happens until then. I look forward to going home to see my loved ones and friends in Heaven. The future for me now is in the present moment—literally. I look forward to whatever God has planned for me each day and only this day.

Whatever I am compelled to do, if it's from my gut and

not my head, I pursue it as I know it's God networking for me. I am fearless today, which is a miracle in itself, and it is so freeing to feel like that. It is impossible for Fear and Faith to live together. Knowing that I am not in control of anything in my life is such a relief I can't begin to articulate it. That was the real reason why I was anorexic. All the years of denying myself joy, being frightened to the point of arrogance, and rejecting the idea that there was something way more powerful than I was, the highest form of pride and self-importance I could have ever known. Something God doesn't want us to be. He wants humbleness and love from us. It's becoming harder by the minute to ignore the violence, hate, and anger in the world today and to not live in this world but of it, but I do all I cannot pay attention to it.

Sure, there will still be obstacles throughout the rest of my life until it's time to go "home," but to know on a physiological level that I am most definitely not alone and connected to God is amazing. I laugh at the obstacles and the hard and painful times now because I know it won't last forever. Nothing ever does. I go to sleep thankful for my day and look up into the clouds and the stars, thanking God for another day and for every moment of the day for this life and everything I've been through and am about to experience. I have glimpses of the old Lisa now and then. It is usually a trigger of something I've not dealt with when this happens. Now, I look at issues that arise in life as blessings. Pain is an opportunity to grow and is a preparation for what He wants us to do next, but having said that, I don't mean go looking for pain; let it happen naturally.

Then, in 2019, I had the idea of writing a cookbook based on the foods of the Bible. Many other stories and movies have been written but not about food and included affirmations and verses to explain why these were eaten and available. But I happily realized while researching this idea many of my recipes already include most of these ingredients. People also appreciated food differently back then, mostly on a spiritual level, because they knew it came from God. They never took that for granted. Food was often scarce as there was no refrigeration and very seasonal (the true "Farm to Table" concept), so I assume a good part of the day was spent sourcing and preparing food. Basic Instructions Before Leaving Earth is how my husband looks at the Bible, and I like that. The biggest message I took away from doing my research was it's mostly about giving and love, and what better way to give than through cooking?

These were my findings and thought you might be interested in what those were. Wine was the most important staple! It is said that God Himself first showed Noah how wine was made. Vineyards and grapes were in abundance in ancient Israel. Many scriptures refer to the importance of wine and warn against drunkenness, which didn't seem to stick! The wine also had to be Kosher; therefore, only the Jewish people were to make the wine. Wine was mostly drunk out of metal goblets or earthenware mugs, except for the poor; they used wooden cups. Glass was very expensive and hard to make. Wine was considered medicinal at the time, too. Water wasn't often pure in wells as they carried bacteria (which is why they preferred spring water instead), which caused soreness and inflammation in the stomach. To fix this, they drank wine to help kill water-borne bacteria.

Bread was an essential, basic food and was treated with great respect. Many rules were created to preserve and show deep respect for this gift from God. Any crumbs left weren't to be thrown away but instead gathered to snack on later. Also, bread was never to be cut but broken apart. Women almost always milled the wheat grains or barley, and because the bread would mold too quickly because of the lack of refrigeration, enough was made for only a day or two. These women were busy! Cow's milk was rarely drunk, as it would go bad too quickly.   Goat milk and ewe were more common. And since milk   soiled quickly, cheese-making was more common. Honey was often used as a sweetener. The bees were colonized like today, resulting in so much honey some of it was exported. Interestingly, cane sugar was unknown at the time in the Holy Land.

Very few eggs were eaten back then, as well. Eggs were mostly reserved for the very wealthy. Chickens were scarce, but the idea of eating poultry seemed to come to light in Jewish regions around 500 BC. Vegetables were the diet of the common people, consisted mostly of vegetables, beans, and lentils, being at the top of the list. Cucumbers and onions were very popular, too.

Meat, as I suspected, was far less consumed back then than today. Meat was mostly eaten by the wealthy, and they ate a great deal of it. When big feasts were approaching, an older animal was chosen and fed grain for several months as they wanted a fatter animal. Goats and lambs were the most common, but occasionally, a cow was chosen. The poor never killed animals unless there was a large family gathering. Because of the shelf life, meat was often pickled or salted.

Fish was more important than meat, making it the most common source of protein. They mostly came from The Sea of Galilee and were imported from the Mediterranean Sea. They often salted fish or pickled it to preserve it, as fish went bad quickly as well. Salt came from the Dead Sea as it was close (I would assume), which also helped preserve certain foods. Black pepper, which is my favorite spice, was very expensive, as was cinnamon, because they had to be imported. Other spices used were capers, cumin, saffron, mustard, coriander, dill, rosemary, garlic, mint, onions, rue, and shallots. Rue is a perennial plant and a member of the same family as the citrus fruits.

Nuts were always available, like walnuts, pistachios, and almonds. And, like today, they were roasted mostly. Okay, so locusts were eaten back then, and this one shocked the heck out of me, if I am to be honest! I've eaten weird things before, but nothing this weird! Apparently, there were 800 different types of edible locusts, which were either boiled or dried in the sun and made into a   powder. The powder was bitter and often added to flour to make a popular bitter biscuit. Who knew?

Olive oil was the fat of that time, and butter was rarely used as it would also go bad in a few days, but olive oil was more common. There were so many olive trees that olives and olive oil had to be exported. Olive oil symbolized strength and health. And finally, fruit. It was a major part of the people's diet as it was also very abundant and exported as well. Melons, figs, pomegranates, dates, and blackberries were at the top of the list. So, I wrote my cookbook, The Thoughtful Chef, and published it in 2022. It's full of important information and clean, healthy recipes. I have so much more to do, God willing.

There is definitely a reason for everything, and the end result of each trial is always for our benefit, even if we can't see it. It can wake us up to a better way of life. Mine, thankfully, did. It's only been since 2012 that I have finally embraced my fingers as a whole part of my body, too, which is huge for me. They are beautiful and artistic, and all by the grace of God. I've accepted the loss, so much so that I rejoice in their imperfectness. I'm so happy I found Him, and I am grateful that He never gave up on me. He was with me my whole life. I just didn't know it. I hope you find your way to supreme bliss while alive on this earth. It's a wonderful feeling.

ABOUT THE AUTHOR

Lisa Stalvey has been cooking now for over forty years, constantly growing in her craft. She had the fortunate experience to train under Wolfgang Puck at Ma Maison in 1979 and went on to work at L'Orangerie and La Toque, ending up as Wolfgang's head chef at Spago in 1986, just seven years into her career.

After three years at Spago, she consulted for several restaurants and finally took a break from cooking and decided to cook privately. Having an opportunity to bring California cuisine to Reykjavik, Iceland, in 1991, and while there, she spoke with the owners (the then-married Jeanette and Rikki Farr) of a new restaurant that was to open in 1992 called Bambu. After four months in Iceland and five weeks in Europe on a food trip, she returned, took the interview, and got the job as executive chef, her first one since the start of my career. While at Bambu, she won three awards for one of the "Top 100 Chefs in America," leading others into culinary expertise approaching the new millennium.

During her last month at Bambu, she was hired by Paul Newman to develop his Newman's Own Steak Sauce and Newman's Own Parisian Salad Dressing for Newman's Own and was commissioned to co-author two cookbooks called Newman's Own Cookbook and The Hole in the

Wall Gang—A Children's Cookbook. During this time, she started a catering business called The Malibu Chef, continuing to cook privately while building her business and delivering healthy meals for families or professionals who don't have time to cook.

For the Love of God and Food covers the first fourteen years of her now forty-fifth year as a professional chef. The story tells of unforeseen circumstances at the very beginning of her career when the unimaginable accident happened.

Her world was swirling at light speed, caught in the hells of her own spiritual and physical starvation.

Lisa has come to understand since this writing that what happened to her was a gift. God was spinning the cocoon for her long journey ahead, creating her rebirth in His way and perfect timing. God saw the bigger picture, as He is the Gardener of our lives, clipping away our weeds and our thorns. In her case, she literally was "pruned."

Lisa's greatest hope is that For the Love of God and Food will help others see that life is beautiful even when things are bad. There is always a reason why things happen that we don't understand. It's never for harm if we take a hard, loving look at why you became addicted in any form, whether it be food-related, alcohol or drug-related, or sexually related.

It is important to always remember that even though

certain experiences may be painful, they are often for our own good. I always knew I'd go through painful things in life, but losing fingers doing what I loved wasn't a remote thought in my head. Life's challenges and hardships can be difficult to endure, for sure, but they definitely serve as catalysts for growth, resilience, and personal development. In the midst of my pain, it was very hard to see the bigger picture or understand the purpose behind my struggle. However, with time and reflection, I came to realize that these difficult moments have shaped me into a stronger, wiser person. This perspective helped me find meaning and purpose through my pain, ultimately leading me to come to God and Jesus with much greater appreciation for the journey of life.

Printed in the USA
CPSIA information can be obtained
at www.ICGtesting.com
LVHW021258100424
776895LV00009BA/164